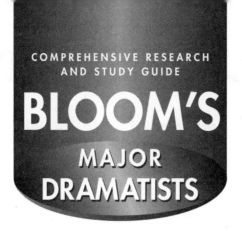

COMPREHENSIVE RESEARCH
AND STUDY GUIDE

BLOOM'S
MAJOR
DRAMATISTS

Shakespeare's Tragedies

EDITED AND WITH AN
INTRODUCTION BY HAROLD BLOOM

BLOOM'S MAJOR DRAMATISTS

Anton Chekhov
Henrik Ibsen
Arthur Miller
Eugene O'Neill
Shakespeare's Comedies
Shakespeare's Histories
Shakespeare's Romances
Shakespeare's Tragedies
George Bernard Shaw
Tennessee Williams

BLOOM'S MAJOR NOVELISTS

Jane Austen
The Brontës
Willa Cather
Charles Dickens
William Faulkner
F. Scott Fitzgerald
Nathaniel Hawthorne
Ernest Hemingway
Toni Morrison
John Steinbeck
Mark Twain
Alice Walker

BLOOM'S MAJOR SHORT STORY WRITERS

William Faulkner
F. Scott Fitzgerald
Ernest Hemingway
O. Henry
James Joyce
Herman Melville
Flannery O'Connor
Edgar Allan Poe
J. D. Salinger
John Steinbeck
Mark Twain
Eudora Welty

BLOOM'S MAJOR WORLD POETS

Geoffrey Chaucer
Emily Dickinson
John Donne
T. S. Eliot
Robert Frost
Langston Hughes
John Milton
Edgar Allan Poe
Shakespeare's Poems & Sonnets
Alfred, Lord Tennyson
Walt Whitman
William Wordsworth

BLOOM'S NOTES

The Adventures of Huckleberry Finn
Aeneid
The Age of Innocence
Animal Farm
The Autobiography of Malcolm X
The Awakening
Beloved
Beowulf
Billy Budd, Benito Cereno, & Bartleby the Scrivener
Brave New World
The Catcher in the Rye
Crime and Punishment
The Crucible

Death of a Salesman
A Farewell to Arms
Frankenstein
The Grapes of Wrath
Great Expectations
The Great Gatsby
Gulliver's Travels
Hamlet
Heart of Darkness & The Secret Sharer
Henry IV, Part One
I Know Why the Caged Bird Sings
Iliad
Inferno
Invisible Man
Jane Eyre
Julius Caesar

King Lear
Lord of the Flies
Macbeth
A Midsummer Night's Dream
Moby-Dick
Native Son
Nineteen Eighty-Four
Odyssey
Oedipus Plays
Of Mice and Men
The Old Man and the Sea
Othello
Paradise Lost
The Portrait of a Lady
A Portrait of the Artist as a Young Man

Pride and Prejudice
The Red Badge of Courage
Romeo and Juliet
The Scarlet Letter
Silas Marner
The Sound and the Fury
The Sun Also Rises
A Tale of Two Cities
Tess of the D'Urbervilles
Their Eyes Were Watching God
To Kill a Mockingbird
Uncle Tom's Cabin
Wuthering Heights

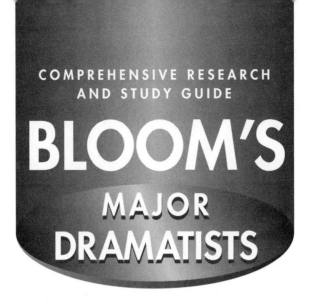

COMPREHENSIVE RESEARCH
AND STUDY GUIDE

BLOOM'S
MAJOR
DRAMATISTS

Shakespeare's Tragedies

EDITED AND WITH AN INTRODUCTION
BY HAROLD BLOOM

Printed and bound in the United States of America.

3 5 7 9 8 6 4 2

Library of Congress Cataloging-in-Publication Data
Shakespeare's tragedies : comprehensive research and study guide /
    edited and with an introduction by Harold Bloom.
        p.   cm. — (Bloom's major dramatists)
    Includes bibliographical references (p.   ) and index.
    ISBN 0-7910-5242-7 (hc)
        1. Shakespeare, William, 1564–1616—Tragedies—Examinations Study
guides.   I. Bloom, Harold.   II. Series
PR2983.S445   1999
822.3′3—dc21   99–29302
                                                                                      CIP

Chelsea House Publishers
1974 Sproul Road, Suite 400
Broomall, PA 19008-0914

The Chelsea House World Wide Web address is
www.chelseahouse.com

Contributing Editor: Mirjana Kalezic

Contents

User's Guide

This volume is designed to present biographical, critical, and bibliographical information on the author's best-known or most important works. Following Harold Bloom's editor's note and introduction are a detailed biography of the playwright, discussing major life events and important literary accomplishments. A plot summary of each play follows, tracing significant themes, patterns, and motifs in the work.

A selection of critical extracts, derived from previously published material from leading critics, analyzes aspects of each play. The extracts consist of statements from the author, if available, early reviews of the work, and later evaluations up to the present. A bibliography of the author's writings (including a complete list of all works written, cowritten, edited, and translated), a list of additional books and articles on the author and his or her work, and an index of themes and ideas in the author's writings conclude the volume.

⁓

Harold Bloom is Sterling Professor of the Humanities at Yale University and Henry W. and Albert A. Berg Professor of English at the New York University Graduate School. He is the author of over 20 books and the editor of more than 30 anthologies of literary criticism.

Professor Bloom's works include *Shelley's Mythmaking* (1959), *The Visionary Company* (1961), *Blake's Apocalypse* (1963), *Yeats* (1970), *A Map of Misreading* (1975), *Kabbalah and Criticism* (1975), and *Agon: Toward a Theory of Revisionism* (1982). *The Anxiety of Influence* (1973) sets forth Professor Bloom's provocative theory of the literary relationships between the great writers and their predecessors. His most recent books include *The American Religion* (1992), *The Western Canon* (1994), *Omens of Millennium: The Gnosis of Angels, Dreams, and Resurrection* (1996), and *Shakespeare: The Invention of the Human* (1998), a finalist for the 1998 National Book Award.

Professor Bloom earned his Ph.D. from Yale University in 1955 and has served on the Yale faculty since then. He is a 1985 MacArthur Foundation Award recipient, served as the Charles Eliot Norton Professor of Poetry at Harvard University in 1987–88, and has received honorary degrees from the universities of Rome and Bologna. In 1999, Professor Bloom received the prestigious American Academy of Arts and Letters Gold Medal for Criticism.

Currently, Harold Bloom is the editor of numerous Chelsea House volumes of literary criticism, including the series BLOOM'S NOTES, BLOOM'S MAJOR SHORT STORY WRITERS, BLOOM'S MAJOR POETS, MAJOR LITERARY CHARACTERS, MODERN CRITICAL VIEWS, MODERN CRITICAL INTERPRETATIONS, AND WOMEN WRITERS OF ENGLISH AND THEIR WORKS.

Editor's Note

The Critical Views throughout favor the central traditions of Shakespeare criticism, from Samuel Johnson, William Hazlitt, and A. C. Bradley, through W. H. Auden, Harold Goddard, and Rosalie Colie, to Graham Bradshaw and Harold Bloom.

The absence here of "French Shakespeare" (Foucault-inspired, deconstructive, ostensibly "feminist" or "Marxist") is amiably deliberate.

Introduction

HAROLD BLOOM

Shakespeare's five major tragedies are widely recognized as among the supreme achievements of Western literature. One can think of the J-Writer's strand of Genesis-Exodus-Numbers, of the *Iliad,* of Dante's *Comedy,* as comparable eminences, together with the principal surviving dramas of Aeschylus, Sophocles, and Euripides. Though it is customary to group Shakespeare's major tragedies, *Hamlet* clearly is in a class of one, since its inwardness is unique, and enigmatic, while *Antony and Cleopatra,* at the other chronological extreme of these masterworks, also stands apart. *Othello, King Lear,* and *Macbeth* have more affinities with one another than with *Hamlet* or *Antony and Cleopatra.*

Hamlet is a radical theatrical experiment, perhaps the most radical we have known. Shakespeare cuts a gap into the play, from Act II, scene two, through Act III, scene two, that ought to destroy any audience's belief in the reality of what is being represented. Since the play co-opts us as accomplices, we accept every bewilderment we are shown. Hamlet himself is displayed as an authorial consciousness, and also as a great hero-villain, loved but unloving and perfectly capable of acting as a casual slaughterer. Yet, despite the well-founded cavils of a few critics, audiences tend to love Hamlet the more intensely even as he demonstrates that he neither wants nor needs such love. William Hazlitt, speaking for the audience, said that we were Hamlet, a fusion that has been endemic for two centuries, and that may never depart. The drama is a "poem unlimited," of no genre really, and its protagonist, who has inspired so many imitators, continues to be an unique figure, the most isolated character in Shakespeare, perhaps indeed in all of Western literature.

Is Hamlet a tragic hero? So various are both the prince and his play that your answer may tell more about you than about Hamlet. Something deeply personal, perhaps familial, enters into this play, whose lost original very likely was by the young Shakespeare himself (though some scholars, on dubious evidence, vote for Thomas Kyd, author of the celebrated *Spanish Tragedy*). Perhaps the deaths of Shakespeare's father and of Hamnet, his only son, are more relevant to *Hamlet* than we know, or perhaps Shakespeare is atoning for an earlier dramatic defeat, though that again is much more than we know.

Hamlet is all that is central to his play; even Claudius and Gertrude seem more peripheral than not. No other consciousness can assert much for itself in Hamlet's charismatic and overwhelming presence. Yet *Othello*, while the Moor's tragedy, is Iago's play, his triumphal march to the psychic and moral annihilation of his superb captain. Iago's malignity is anything but motiveless. He has been passed over for promotion by his war-god, Othello, and this partial rejection has been a vastation for the ensign or flag-officer, loyally pledged to perish rather than permit Othello's colors to be taken in battle. John Milton, involuntarily Shakespeare's closest student, made his Satan into a disciple of Iago. Satan's Sense of Injured Merit is precisely Iago's, but Othello is considerably more vulnerable than Milton's God. Othello falls, and only Emilia, at the price of her life, prevents Iago's absolute triumph.

Shakespeare wrote *King Lear, Macbeth,* and *Antony and Cleoptra* in a continuous burst of creativity for fourteen consecutive months. I cannot think of anything comparable in the history of literature. *King Lear,* though very oddly handled by recent politicized critics, is the most awesome poetic drama that I know. It is a great dance of contraries, a quarrel between sublimity and human clay. Whether the character of King Lear is too grand for the stage, as Charles Lamb argued, is hardly a popular question these days, but remains pragmatically quite real to me, as I have never seen an actor wholly adequate to the role. Shakespeare risked a tragedy beyond limits, and yet we have no choice but to share in the play's extravagance. No other drama seems to me to make such large demands upon an audience.

Macbeth emanates out of cosmological emptiness akin to *King Lear*'s. In both plays, we have been thrown into realms that touch the limits of nature. Macbeth himself, more even than Lear, becomes a theater open to the night-sky, and to the forces that ride the air. What is most surprising and most sublime about *Macbeth* is that we cannot separate ourselves from the hero-villain, no matter how deeply he recedes into his heart of darkness. Shakespeare lavished intellect upon Hamlet and spirit upon Lear, but no one else receives so vast an imaginative endowment as does Macbeth. The paradox, tragically ironic, is that this man of blood is Shakespeare's greatest poet.

After the enormities of *King Lear* and *Macbeth,* Shakespeare breaks out into the world that destroys Antony and Cleopatra, whose heroic era dies with them. Though a double tragedy, *Antony and Cleopatra* is also a joyous display of Shakespeare's art at its most comprehensive. The largeness of personality in both Cleopatra and Antony is answered by the psychic and representational largeness of the play. Shakespeare's superb panoply of gifts, as comprehensive and generous as ever has been offered to us, come together in *Antony and Cleopatra* with a splendor that Shakespeare never sought again.

Biography of
William Shakespeare

William Shakespeare was born in Stratford-on-Avon in April 1564 into a family of some prominence. His father, John Shakespeare, was a glover and merchant of leather goods, who earned enough to marry the daughter of his father's landlord, Mary Arden, in 1557. John Shakespeare was a prominent citizen in Stratford, and at one point, he served as an alderman and bailiff.

Shakespeare presumably attended the Stratford grammar school, where he would have received an education in Latin, but he did not go on to either Oxford or Cambridge universities. Little is recorded about Shakespeare's early life; indeed, the first record of his life after his christening is of his marriage to Anne Hathaway in 1582 in the church at Temple Grafton, near Stratford. He would have been required to obtain a special license from the bishop as security that there was no impediment to the marriage. Peter Alexander states in his book *Shakespeare's Life and Art* that marriage at this time in England required neither a church nor a priest or, for that matter, even a document—only a declaration of the contracting parties in the presence of witnesses. Thus, it was customary, though not mandatory, to follow the marriage with a church ceremony.

Little is known about William and Anne Shakespeare's marriage. Their first child, Susanna, was born in May 1583, and twins, Hamnet and Judith Shakespeare, in 1585. Later on, Susanna married Dr. John Hall, but the younger daughter, Judith, remained unmarried. When Hamnet died in Stratford in 1596, the boy was only eleven years old.

We have no record of Shakespeare's activities for the seven years after the birth of his twins, but by 1592 he was in London working as an actor. He was also apparently well-known as a playwright, for reference is made of him by his contemporary, Robert Greene, in *A Groatsworth of Wit*, as "an upstart crow."

Several companies of actors were in London at this time. Shakespeare may have had connection with one or more of them before 1592, but we have no record that tells us definitely. However, we do know of his long association with the most famous and successful troupe, the Lord Chamberlain's Men. (When James I came to the throne in 1603, after Elizabeth's death, the troupe's name changed to the King's Men.) In 1599 the Lord Chamberlain's Men provided the financial backing for the construction of their own theatre, the Globe.

The Globe was begun by a carpenter named James Burbage and finished by his two sons, Cuthbert and Robert. To escape the jurisdiction of the Corporation of London, which was composed of conservative Puritans who opposed the theatre's "licentiousness," James Burbage built the Globe just outside London, in the Liberty of Holywell, beside Finsbury Fields. This also meant that the Globe was safer from the threats that lurked in London's crowded streets, like plague and other diseases, as well as rioting mobs. When James Burbage died in 1598, his sons completed the Globe's construction. Shakespeare played a vital role, financially and otherwise, in the construction of the theater, which was finally occupied some time before May 16, 1599.

Shakespeare not only acted with the Globe's company of actors; he was also a shareholder and eventually became the troupe's most important playwright. The company included London's most famous actors, who inspired the creation of Shakespeare's well-known characters such as Hamlet and Lear, as well as his clowns and fools.

In his early years, however, Shakespeare did not confine himself to the theatre. He also composed some mythological-erotic poetry, such as *Venus and Adonis* and *The Rape of Lucrece,* both of which were dedicated to the earl of Southampton. Shakespeare was successful enough that in 1597 he was able to purchase his own home in Stratford, New Place. He could even call himself a gentleman, for his father had been granted a coat of arms.

By 1598 Shakespeare had written some of his most famous works, *Romeo and Juliet, The Comedy of Errors, A Midsummer Night's Dream, The Merchant of Venice, Two Gentleman of Verona,* and *Love's Labor Lost,* as well as his historical plays *Richard II, Richard III, Henry IV,* and *King John.* Somewhere around the turn of the century, Shakespeare wrote his romantic comedies, *As You Like It, Twelfth Night,* and *Much Ado About Nothing,* as well as *Henry V,* the last of his history plays in the Prince Hal series. During the next 10 years he wrote his great tragedies, *Hamlet, Macbeth, Othello, King Lear,* and *Antony and Cleopatra.*

At this time, the theatre was burgeoning in London; the public took an avid interest in drama, the audiences were large, the plays demonstrated an enormous range of variety, and playwrights competed for approval. By 1613, however, the rising tide of Puritanism had changed the theatre. With the desertion of the theatres by the middle classes, the acting companies were compelled to depend more on the aristocracy, which also meant that they now had to cater to a more sophisticated audience.

Perhaps this change in London's artistic atmosphere contributed to Shakespeare's reasons for leaving London in 1610. His retirement from the theatre is sometimes thought to be evidence that his artistic skills were waning. During this time, however, he wrote *The Tempest* and *Henry VIII.* He also wrote the "tragicomedies," *Pericles, Cymbeline,* and *The Winter's Tale.* These were thought to be inspired by Shakespeare's personal problems, and have sometimes been considered proof of his greatly diminished abilities.

However, so far as biographical facts indicate, the circumstances of his life at this time do not imply any personal problems. He was in good health, financially secure, and enjoyed an excellent reputation. Indeed, although he was settled in Stratford at this time, he made frequent visits to London, enjoying and participating in events at the royal court, directing rehearsals, and attending to other business matters.

In addition to his brilliant and enormous contributions to the theatre, Shakespeare remained a poetic genius throughout the years, publishing a well-renowned and critically-acclaimed sonnet cycle in 1609. Shakespeare's contributions to this popular poetic genre are all the more amazing in his break with contemporary notions of subject matter. Shakespeare idealized the beauty of man as an object of praise and devotion (rather than the Petrarchan tradition of the idealized, unattainable woman). In the same spirit of breaking with tradition, Shakespeare also treated themes which hitherto had been considered off limits—the dark, sexual side of a woman as opposed to the Petrarchan ideal of a chaste and remote love object. He also expanded the sonnet's emotional range, including such emotions as delight, pride, shame, disgust, sadness, and fear.

When Shakespeare died in 1616, no collected edition of his works had ever been published, although some of his plays had been printed in separate unauthorized editions. (Some of these were taken from his manuscripts, some from the actors' prompt books, and others were reconstructed from memory by actors or spectators.) In 1623, two members of the King's Men, John Hemings and Henry Condell, published a collection of all the plays they considered to be authentic, the First Folio.

Included in the First Folio is a poem by Shakespeare's contemporary Ben Jonson, an outstanding playwright and critic in his own right. Jonson paid tribute to Shakespeare's genius, proclaiming his superiority to what previously had been held as the models for literary excellence—the Greek and Latin writers. "Triumph, my Britain, thou hast one to show / To whom all scenes of Europe homage owe. / He was not of an age, but for all time!"

Jonson was the first to state what has been said so many times since. Having captured what is permanent and universal to all human beings at all times, Shakespeare's genius continues to inspire us—and the critical debate about his works never ceases.

Plot Summary of
Hamlet

The Tragedy of Hamlet, Prince of Denmark, opens in **Act I** at the royal castle of Elsinore, where Horatio joins Marcellus and Bernardo, the guards on their watch, to investigate the truth of their reports of a ghastly apparition of the late King of Denmark. As Horatio and the guards discuss the threat of Fortinbras, commander of the Norwegian brigades, the ghost appears, but Horatio cannot persuade him to speak before the rooster's crow announces the dawn. Horatio and the watchmen agree that young Hamlet, the dead King's son, should be informed of this phenomenon and should join the watch the following evening.

In scene two, King Claudius, King of Denmark, expresses his thanks to his counselors (who include Polonius, Laertes, Voltemand, and Cornelius) for assisting in two recent ceremonies: his brother's funeral and his marriage to his brother's wife, Gertrude. He then sends his ambassadors to the King of Norway to ask him to mollify his nephew Fortinbras's ambition to invade and recover lands lost by his father. Young Laertes, son of Claudius' counselor Polonius, asks for permission to return to France, which Claudius grants.

Claudius then addresses young Hamlet with the words, "But now, my cousin Hamlet, and my son—"at which Hamlet, seizing on the words "cousin" and "son," responds, "A little more than kin, and less than kind." This is Hamlet's first comment, and it immediately draws the audience's attention. Gertrude and Claudius ask Hamlet to stay in Denmark and he agrees.

When the court departs, it leaves Hamlet alone on the stage and he delivers his first of four soliloquies ("O that this too too solid flesh would melt/ thaw and resolve itself into a dew . . . "), praising his father's excellence, which is to Claudius's as "Hyperion to satyr." This speech reveals Hamlet's abhorrence for his mother's hasty marriage to his uncle. The soliloquies allow Shakespeare to take us into Hamlet's mind, giving us an awareness of his internal being.

Horatio, Marcellus, and Bernardo enter and tell Hamlet about the ghost. He agrees to join them at the watch that night.

The third scene shows Laertes bidding farewell to his sister Ophelia. He warns her not to take Hamlet's affections seriously. Their father, Polonius, makes an entrance, and fearing that Hamlet's affection is not sincere, he orders Ophelia not to see him anymore. Ophelia yields to her father's wish.

In scene four, night falls and Hamlet and Horatio accompany the guards on their watch. To Hamlet's astonishment, the ghost appears and beckons to him. Although his friends try to dissuade him, fearing that the ghost is actually an evil spirit, Hamlet follows the ghost.

Scene five is set at another part of the battlements, where the ghost reveals himself as the spirit of old Hamlet and unfolds his story. In graphic language, he tells how Claudius poisoned him while he was asleep and seduced his wife. He asks Hamlet to avenge his death but not to harm Gertrude. After the ghost's last words, "Remember me," Hamlet vows that he will execute swift vengeance. He refuses to tell his friends what has taken place and asks them three times to swear on his sword that they will disclose nothing of what they have witnessed. He also intimates that he may "put an antic disposition"; in other words, he is warning them that his future behavior may appear foolish and crazy.

In the first scene of **Act II,** Polonius tells an attendant to spy on his son's activities in France in order to determine if he is leading too wild a life. Ophelia enters and relates that she has seen Hamlet in her chamber and that his behavior frightened her. Polonius surmises that the cause of Hamlet's lunacy is his love for Ophelia and rushes to report the matter to the King.

In the meantime, Claudius and Gertrude welcome Rosencrantz and Guildenstern, friends of Hamlet, who are summoned by the king to find out the cause of Hamlet's distress. The ambassadors from Norway bring good news. Fortinbras will not attack Denmark but will attack Poland instead and asks for permission to pass through Denmark to do so.

Claudius is unconvinced by Polonius's theory that unrequited love has triggered some weakness in Hamlet's mind. Meanwhile, as soon as Hamlet sees his friends Rosencrantz and Guildenstern he suspects they are Claudius's spies. With the company of players that arrive, Hamlet arranges a play, "The Murder of Gonzago," with "some dozen or sixteen lines" that he will insert. Left alone on the stage, in his second soliloquy ("O what a rogue and peasant slave am I!"), he expresses self-contempt at his lack of passion for avenging his father's death.

In **Act III,** scene one, Rosencrantz and Guildenstern have little to report to Claudius except that the prince has expressed great interest in the actors and has asked for the King's presence at one of their performances. Polonius attempts to set a meeting between Ophelia and Hamlet. With Claudius and Polonius spying from afar, Hamlet enters and begins his third soliloquy ("To be, or not to be, that is the question") in reaction to the passion expressed by an actor while reciting Hecuba's speech. In this speech Hamlet shows both profound insight and intense emotion.

When Ophelia appears he greets her kindly, but when she returns his gifts, he begins railing against women. He urges Ophelia to go to a nunnery and not to be a breeder of sinners. Baffled by his tirades, Ophelia exclaims "O what a noble mind is here o'erthrown!" Claudius and Polonius disagree in interpretations of Hamlet's behavior. Polonius still thinks that the cause lies in love, whereas Claudius is convinced that Hamlet's presence is dangerous.

In scene two, Hamlet seems once more in possession of his full faculties while he advises the players how to act. Claudius and the royal auditors assemble to see the play; Hamlet sits next to Ophelia. The players enact a scene that resembles the one that the ghost had told Hamlet. By watching Claudius during the performance, Hamlet hopes to discover the truth for himself.

His plan works perfectly. Claudius becomes so unnerved that he walks out before the end of the scene and calls for lights. Hamlet and Horatio discuss the King's behavior, and Hamlet, now convinced by Claudius' reaction, has no reason to delay his revenge. By the end of the scene, Rosencrantz and Guildenstern announce the Queen's wish to see Hamlet in her chamber.

In the third scene, Claudius instructs Rosencrantz and Guildenstern to accompany Hamlet to England. Polonius tells the King that Hamlet is heading to Gertrude's room, and he promises he'll hide behind a tapestry to eavesdrop on their conversation. Left alone, Claudius kneels down to pray. Hamlet comes upon the King but fails to take advantage of the opportunity to kill him. He rationalizes that if he kills him at prayer he would send him to heaven.

In the next scene, however, Hamlet proves he is capable of murder. He faces Gertrude in her room and talks to her in such a wild manner that she becomes frightened for her safety. Polonius, who was eavesdropping behind the curtain, is alarmed and calls for help. Hamlet stabs him through the curtain. Ignoring the body of Polonius, Hamlet rails at his mother for marrying Claudius, but the ghost appears to remind him of his "blunted purpose." Hamlet's conversation with the ghost, who is invisible to Gertrude (although Horatio and the guards did see him in the first act), is further proof of her son's lunacy. Hamlet protests that he is not mad. His parting words reveal his speculation about the treachery hidden in the King's order to send him to England. Hamlet departs, dragging Polonius's corpse.

In **Act IV**, scene one, Gertrude describes Hamlet's killing of Polonius to Claudius, who immediately sends Rosencrantz and Guildenstern after Hamlet. In scene two, Hamlet mocks Rosencrantz and Guildenstern when they question him about Polonius. He runs away, playing hide and seek, and forces them to pursue him. When brought before Claudius in the third scene, Hamlet returns to his "antic" manner. The King uses Hamlet's slaying of Polonius as the pretext to dispatch him to England, along with sealed orders that call for Hamlet's death as soon as he arrives.

Scene four shows Hamlet and his escort heading toward the coast, passing Fortinbras and his army on their way to Poland. In his fourth soliloquy ("How all occasion do inform against me/ and spur my dull revenge!"), Hamlet, astonished that so many men will risk their lives for so little, contrasts his own inaction with the fearlessness of thousands of troops.

In scene five, the Queen is told that Ophelia has gone mad after her father's death. Ophelia is shown singing snatches of ballads and speaking in incomprehensible fragments. In the meantime, Laertes has received news of his father's death and gathers a rabble of supporters to avenge it at any cost. He forces his way into the castle, but the King is able to calm him down and takes him away to talk secretly about his revenge. The contrast between Hamlet and Laertes is regularly remarked upon by critics: while Laertes's desire for revenge is irrepressible, Hamlet's hesitates, reluctant to act.

In scene six, sailors arrive bringing a letter from Hamlet to Horatio. In it, Hamlet reports his capture by pirates and his return to Denmark. He also tells Horatio where he can find him. In the next scene, Claudius receives a letter from Hamlet as well while he is conferring with Laertes. Claudius realizes that he has failed to dispose of Hamlet and he persuades Laertes to take part in a plot to murder the prince. According to the plan, Laertes will poison the tip of his sword, and Claudius will put a cup of poisoned wine within Hamlet's reach in case Laertes fails. At this point, Gertrude enters and reports that Ophelia has drowned herself.

Act V begins in a graveyard where Horatio and Hamlet come upon two gravediggers. A funeral party, which includes the King and Queen and Laertes, enters and Hamlet discovers that the grave is for Ophelia. Laertes laments melodramatically over his sister's body, even leaps into the grave and asks to be buried with her. That demonstration of feelings triggers something in Hamlet, who tries to match Laertes's ranting. The King tries to keep the situation under control.

In the second scene, Hamlet tells Horatio about his escape and the forged letter in which he asks for the execution of Rosencrantz and Guildenstern. The courtier Osric announces that Claudius is wagering on Hamlet's skill at the fencing match against Laertes. Despite a certain foreboding, Hamlet agrees to the match.

At the beginning of the duel, Hamlet scores two hits. While watching, Gertrude drinks the poisoned wine that had been intended for her son. The second part of the plot is successful, as Laertes stabs Hamlet with a poison rapier, but Hamlet manages to exchange weapons and wounds Laertes with the deadly sword in return. When the Queen dies, Laertes, understanding that he, too, will die from the poison, confesses the plot and implicates the King. Hamlet stabs Claudius and forces him to drink the poisoned wine. After Laertes and Claudius die, Hamlet insists that Horatio live to tell his story and clean his "wounded name"; he gives his dying words to Fortinbras, who arrives on his way from Poland to become the successor to the Danish throne.

Critics have debated endlessly the meaning of the prince's last words: "The rest is silence." ❀

List of Characters in
Hamlet

Hamlet, Prince of Denmark, has been called the "melancholy Dane" and "a sweet Prince." His father's ghost shatters Hamlet's character when he gives him the task of revenge. Hamlet is presented as a rare combination of traits: affectionate, free, modest, truthful, as well as ironic, hateful, cruel—and all these traits are veiled by his critical intellect, his melancholic broodings, his sensuality, and his hesitancy.

Old Hamlet is Hamlet's father, whom Claudius murdered before the beginning of the play. His ghost appears and demands that Hamlet avenge the murder. His last words on the first meeting are: "Remember me." Later he reappears to Hamlet when he seems to be about to hurt his mother. The ghost's words this time are: "Do not forget."

Claudius is Hamlet's uncle. He becomes the king of Denmark by murdering Hamlet's father. Hamlet describes him best by contrasting his father to him: "So excellent a king, that was to this/Hyperion to a satyr." Claudius doesn't admit his guilt until the third act, when Shakespeare presents Claudius' agonized conscience in tortuous speech during his prayer. Hamlet kills him in the last act of the play.

Gertrude is Hamlet's mother, and as the drama opens, the wife of Claudius, whom she has married only a month after the murder of Hamlet's father. "Frailty, thy name is woman" is Hamlet's remark. She is accidentally killed at the end of the play when she drinks from the poisoned cup meant for her son.

Horatio is a faithful friend and confidant of Hamlet, presented as a composed character, "more an antique Roman than a Dane." As Hamlet dies, Horatio wants to commit suicide, but Hamlet pleads with him to clear his "wounded name."

Polonius is the father of Ophelia and Laertes, and advisor to Claudius. He eavesdrops for Claudius in a prearranged meeting between Hamlet and Ophelia. When he shouts for help, hidden behind the arras in Gertrude's closet, Hamlet runs his sword through the curtain and the figure behind it. He is presented as a busybody who misinterprets almost everything.

Ophelia is the daughter of Polonius and the sister to Laertes. Hamlet has wooed her but she obeys her father's wish to discourage the prince's declarations of love. She goes mad after her father has been killed and drowns herself. The Shakespeare scholar and biographer Dr. Samuel Johnson found her "the young, the beautiful, the harmless, and the pious." A question has always puzzled critics: Does Hamlet love her?

Laertes is the son of Polonius and the brother of Ophelia. At the beginning of the play he goes to France, but he returns to Denmark to avenge his father's death. He is presented as a revenger without scruple, unhesitant and brutal. He plans Hamlet's death with Claudius. In the final scene he confesses his deceit before he meets his death: the rapier he has wounded Hamlet with—and in turn has been wounded by—is poisoned.

Fortinbras is the nephew of the king of Norway, who plans to regain by force the lands his father lost to Old Hamlet. Instead, he leads his troops to Poland. He arrives at the end of the play when the whole Danish royal family is dead. Hamlet gives his "dying voice" to him and he becomes a king. Fortinbras, like Laertes, is presented as a man of action and functions as a foil for Hamlet.

Rosencrantz and **Guildenstern** are an inseparable pair, Hamlet's old friends. Claudius orders them to find out the cause of Hamlet's melancholy. Hamlet steals the letters containing orders for his execution, and he replaces them with forged letters ordering their death instead. As the play comes to a close, an ambassador from England arrives with news that the pair have been executed.❀

Critical Views on
Hamlet

SAMUEL JOHNSON ON HAMLET'S VARIETY

[Dr. Samuel Johnson (1709–1784), one of the outstanding British literary figures of the eighteenth century, was a poet, essayist, critic, journalist, and lexicographer. His *Dictionary of the English Language* (1755) was the first major English dictionary to use historical quotations. In 1765 he wrote a monograph, *Preface to His Edition of Shakespeare,* and in the same year he edited a landmark annotated edition of Shakespeare's works. In this short extract, Johnson praises the variety of Hamlet.]

If the dramas of Shakespeare were to be characterised, each by the particular excellence which distinguishes it from the rest, we must allow to the tragedy of *Hamlet* the praise of variety. The incidents are so numerous, that the argument of the play would make a long tale. The scenes are interchangeably diversified with merriment and solemnity; with merriment that includes judicious and instructive observations, and solemnity, not strained by poetical violence above the natural sentiments of man. New characters appear from time to time in continual succession, exhibiting various forms of life and particular modes of conversation. The pretended madness of Hamlet causes much mirth, the mournful distraction of Ophelia fills the heart with tenderness, and every personage produces the effect intended, from the apparition that in the first act chills the blood with horror, to the fop in the last, that exposes affectation to just contempt.

The conduct is perhaps not wholly secure against objections. The action is indeed for the most part in continual progression, but there are some scenes which neither forward nor retard it. Of the feigned madness of Hamlet there appears no adequate cause, for he does nothing which he might not have done with the reputation of sanity. He plays the madman most, when he treats Ophelia with so much rudeness, which seems to be useless and wanton cruelty.

Hamlet is, through the whole play, rather an instrument than an agent. After he has, by the stratagem of the play, convicted the King, he makes no attempt to punish him, and his death is at last effected by an incident which Hamlet has no part in producing.

The catastrophe is not very happily produced; the exchange of weapons is rather an expedient of necessity, than a stroke of art. A scheme might easily have been formed, to kill Hamlet with the dagger, and Laertes with the bowl.

The poet is accused of having shewn little regard to poetical justice, and may be charged with equal neglect of poetical probability. The apparition left the regions of the dead to little purpose; the revenge which he demands is not obtained but by the death of him that was required to take it; and the gratification which would arise from the destruction of an usurper and a murderer, is abated by the untimely death of Ophelia, the young, the beautiful, the harmless, and the pious.

—Samuel Johnson, *The Plays of William Shakespeare* (London: J. & R. Tonson, 1765).

JOHANN WOLFGANG VON GOETHE ON WILLIAM MEISTER AND HAMLET

[Johann Wolfgang von Goethe (1749–1832), the greatest figure of the German Romantic period, was poet, novelist, playwright, and philosopher. Among his many works are the novel *The Sorrows of Young Werther* (1774), the play *Torquato Tasso* (1790), and the poetic work *Roman Elegies* (1795). In his last years Goethe wrote *Wilhelm Meister's Travels* (1821–29) and completed his greatest drama, *Faust* (Part I published 1808; Part II, 1832). In this extract taken from his novel *Wilhelm Meister's Apprenticeship* (1795–96), Goethe depicts the young Wilhelm Meister becoming fascinated with the character of Hamlet.]

⟨Wilhelm Meister:⟩ "I set about investigating every trace of Hamlet's character, as it had shown itself before his father's death: I endeavoured to distinguish what in it was independent of this mournful event; independent of the terrible events that followed; and what most probably the young man would have been, had no such thing occurred.

"Soft, and from a noble stem, this royal flower had sprung up under the immediate influences of majesty: the idea of moral rectitude with that of princely elevation, the feeling of the good and dignified with the consciousness of high birth, had in him been unfolded simultaneously. He was a prince, by birth a prince; and he wished to reign, only that good men might be good without obstruction. Pleasing in form, polished by nature, courteous from the heart, he was meant to be the pattern of youth and the joy of the world.

"Without any prominent passion, his love for Ophelia was a still presentiment of sweet wants. His zeal in knightly accomplishments was not entirely his own; it needed to be quickened and inflamed by praise bestowed on others for excelling in them. Pure in sentiment, he knew the honourable-minded, and could prize the rest which an upright spirit tastes on the bosom of a friend. To a certain degree, he had learned to discern and value the good and the beautiful in arts and sciences; the mean, the vulgar was offensive to him; and if hatred could take root in his tender soul, it was only so far as to make him properly despise the false and changeful insects of a court, and play with them in easy scorn. He was calm in his temper, artless in his conduct; neither pleased with idleness, nor too violently eager for employment. The routine of a university he seemed to continue when at court. He possessed more mirth of humour than of heart; he was a good companion, pliant, courteous, discreet, and able to forget and forgive an injury; yet never able to unite himself with those who overstept the limits of the right, the good, and the becoming ⟨ . . . ⟩.

"Ambition and the love of rule are not the passions that inspire him. As a king's son he would have been contented; but now he is first constrained to consider the difference which separates a sovereign from a subject. The crown was not hereditary; yet a longer possession of it by his father would have strengthened the pretensions of an only son, and secured his hopes of the succession. In place of this, he now beholds himself excluded by his uncle, in spite of specious promises, most probably forever. He is now poor in goods and favour, and a stranger in the scene which from youth he had looked upon as his inheritance. His temper here assumes its first mournful tinge. He feels that now he is not more, that he is less, than a private nobleman; he offers himself as the servant of every one; he is not courteous and condescending, he is needy and degraded.

"His past condition he remembers as a vanished dream. It is in vain that his uncle strives to cheer him, to present his situation in another point of view. The feeling of his nothingness will not leave him.

"The second stroke that came upon him wounded deeper, bowed still more. It was the marriage of his mother. The faithful tender son had yet a mother, when his father passed away. He hoped, in the company of his surviving noble-minded parent, to reverence the heroic form of the departed; but his mother too he loses, and it is something worse than death that robs him of her. The trustful image, which a good child loves to form of its parents, is gone. With the dead there is no help; on the living no hold. She also is a woman, and her name is Frailty, like that of all her sex.⟨ . . . ⟩

"Figure to yourselves this youth," cried he, "this son of princes; conceive him vividly, bring his state before your eyes, and then observe him when he learns that his father's spirit walks; stand by him in the terrors of the night, when the venerable ghost itself appears before him. A horrid shudder passes over him; he speaks to the mysterious form; he sees it beckon him; he follows it, and hears. The fearful accusation of his uncle rings in his ears; the summons to revenge, and the piercing oft-repeated prayer, Remember me!

"And when the ghost has vanished, who is it that stands before us? A young hero panting for vengeance? A prince by birth, rejoicing to be called to punish the usurper of his crown? No! trouble and astonishment take hold of the solitary young man; he grows bitter against smiling villains, swears that he will not forget the spirit, and concludes with the significant ejaculation:

> That time is out of joint: O cursed spite,
> That ever I was born to set it right!

"In these words, I imagine, will be found the key to Hamlet's whole procedure. To me it is clear that Shakspeare meant, in the present case, to represent the effects of a great action laid upon a soul unfit for the performance of it. In this view the whole piece seems to me to be composed. There is an oak-tree planted in a costly jar, which should have borne only pleasant flowers in its bosom; the roots expand, the jar is shivered.

"A lovely, pure, noble and most moral nature, without the strength of nerve which forms a hero, sinks beneath a burden which it cannot bear and must not cast away. All duties are holy for him; the present is too hard. Impossibilities have been required of him; not in themselves impossibilities, but such for him. He winds, and turns, and torments himself; he advances and recoils; is ever put in mind, ever puts himself in mind; at last does all but lose his purpose from his thoughts; yet still without recovering his peace of mind."

—Johann Wolfgang von Goethe, *Wilhelm Meister's Apprenticeship and Travels* [1795–96], vol. 4, translated by Thomas Carlyle (New York: Scribner's, 1904).

August Wilhelm von Schlegel on Hamlet's Flaws

[German scholar and critic August Wilhelm von Schlegel (1767–1845) was one of the most influential advocates of the German Romantic movement. He was also an Orientalist and a poet. His greatest achievement is his translation of Shakespeare. In his famous book *Lectures on Dramatic Art and Literature* (1809–11), excerpted here, Schlegel disagrees with Goethe's praise of Hamlet, finding many flaws in his character.]

With respect to Hamlet's character: I cannot, as I understand the poet's views, pronounce altogether so favourable a sentence upon it as Goethe does. He is, it is true, of a highly cultivated mind, a prince of royal manners, endowed with the finest sense of propriety, susceptible of noble ambition, and open in the highest degree to an enthusiastic admiration of that excellence in others of which he himself is deficient. He acts the part of madness with unrivalled power, convincing the persons who are sent to examine into his supposed loss of reason, merely by telling them unwelcome truths, and rallying them with the most caustic wit. But in the resolutions which he so often embraces and always leaves unexecuted, his weakness is too apparent: he does himself only justice when he implies that there is no greater dissimilarity than between himself and Hercules. He is not solely impelled by necessity to artifice and dissimulation, he has a natural inclination for crooked ways; he is a hypocrite towards himself; his far-fetched scruples are often mere pretexts to cover his want of determination: thoughts, as he says on a different occasion, which have

> but one part wisdom
> And ever three parts coward.

He has been chiefly condemned both for his harshness in repulsing the love of Ophelia, which he himself had cherished, and for his insensibility at her death. But he is too much overwhelmed with his own sorrow to have any compassion to spare for others; besides his outward indifference gives us by no means the measure of his internal perturbation. On the other hand, we evidently perceive in him a malicious joy, when he has succeeded in getting rid of his enemies, more though necessity and accident, which alone are able to impel him to quick and decisive measures, than by the merit of his own courage, as he himself confesses after the murder of Polonius, and with respect to Rosencrantz and Guildenstern. Hamlet has no firm belief either in himself or in anything else: from expressions of religious confidence he passes over to sceptical doubts; he believes in the Ghost of his father as long as he sees it, but as soon as it has disappeared, it appears to him almost in the light of a deception. He has even gone so far as to say, "there is nothing either good or bad, but thinking makes it so;" with him the poet loses himself here in labyrinths of thought, in which neither end nor beginning is discoverable. The stars themselves, from the course of events, afford no answer to the question so urgently proposed to them. A voice from another world, commissioned it would appear, by heaven, demands vengeance for a monstrous enormity, and the demand remains without effect; the criminals are at last punished, but, as it were, by an accidental blow, and not in the solemn way requisite to convey to the world a warning example of justice; irresolute foresight, cunning treachery, and impetuous rage, hurry on to a common destruction; the less guilty and the innocent are equally involved in the general ruin. The destiny of humanity is there exhibited as a gigantic Sphinx, which threatens to precipitate into the abyss of scepticism all who are unable to solve her dreadful enigmas.

—August Wilhelm von Schlegel, *Lectures in Dramatic Art and Literature* [1809], translated by John Black [1816], revised by A. S. W. Morrison (London: George Bell & Sons, 1894): pp. 405–406.

[William Hazlitt (1778–1830) is an English writer best remembered for his essays. Among his many works are *Lectures on the English Poets* (1818), *Lectures on the English Comic Writers* (1819), and *Liber Amoris,* in which he describes the suffering of a love affair that ended disastrously. In this extract taken from his *Characters of Shakespear's Plays* (1817), Hazlitt speaks about Hamlet's power of action.]

The character of Hamlet stands quite by itself. It is not a character marked by strength of will or even of passion, but by refinement of thought and sentiment. Hamlet is as little of the hero as a man can well be: but he is a young and princely novice, full of high enthusiasm and quick sensibility—the sport of circumstances, questioning with fortune and refining on his own feelings, and forced from the natural bias of his disposition by the strangeness of his situation. He seems incapable of deliberate action, and is only hurried into extremities on the spur of the occasion, when he has no time to reflect, as in the scene where he kills Polonius, and again, where he alters the letters which Rosencraus and Guildenstern are taking with them to England, purporting his death. At other times, when he is most bound to act, he remains puzzled, undecided, and sceptical, dallies with his purposes, till the occasion is lost, and finds out some pretence to relapse into indolence and thoughtfulness again. For this reason he refuses to kill the King when he is at his prayers, and by a refinement in malice, which is in truth only an excuse for his own want of resolution, defers his revenge to a more fatal opportunity, when he shall be engaged in some act "that has no relish of salvation in it."

> "He kneels and prays,
> And now I'll do't, and so he goes to heaven,
> And so am I reveng'd: *that would be scann'd.*
> He kill'd my father, and for that,
> I, his sole son, send him to heaven.
> Why this is reward, not revenge.
> Up sword and know thou a more horrid time
> When he is drunk, asleep, or in a rage."

He is the prince of philosophical speculators; and because he cannot have his revenge perfect, according to the most refined idea his wish can form, he declines it altogether. So he scruples to trust the suggestions of the host, contrives the scene of the play to have surer proof of his uncle's guilt, and then rests satisfied with this confirmation of his suspicions, and the success of his experiment, instead of acting upon it. Yet he is sensible of his own weakness, taxes himself with it, and tries to reason himself out of it.

> "How all occasions do inform against me,
> And spur my dull revenge! What is a man,

If his chief good and market of his time
Be but to sleep and feed? A beast; no more.
Sure he that made us with such large discourse,
Looking before and after, gave us not
That capability and god-like reason
To rust in us unus'd. Now whether it be
Bestial oblivion, or some craven scruple
Of thinking too precisely on th' event,—
A thought which quarter'd, hath but one part wisdom,
And ever three parts coward;—I do not know
Why yet I live to say, this thing's to do;
Sith I have cause, and will, and strength, and means
To do it. Examples gross as earth exhort me:
Witness this army of such mass and charge,
Led by a delicate and tender prince,
Whose spirit with divine ambition puff'd,
Makes mouths at the invisible event,
Exposing what is mortal and unsure
To all that fortune, death, and danger dare,
Even for an egg-shell. 'Tis not to be great
Never to stir without great argument;
But greatly to find quarrel in a straw,
When honour's at the stake. How stand I then,
That have a father kill'd, a mother stain'd,
Excitements of my reason and my blood,
And let all sleep, while to my shame I see
The imminent death of twenty thousand men,
That for a fantasy and trick of fame,
Go to their graves like beds, fight for a plot
Whereon the numbers cannot try the cause,
Which is not tomb enough and continent
To hide the slain?—O, from this time forth,
My thoughts be bloody or be nothing worth.

Still he does nothing; and this very speculation on his own infirmity only affords him another occasion for indulging it. It is not from any want of attachment to his father or of abhorrence of his murder that Hamlet is thus dilatory, but it is more to his taste to indulge his imagination in reflecting upon the enormity of the crime and refining on his schemes of vengeance, than to put them into immediate practice. His ruling passion is to think, not to act: and any vague pretext that flatters this propensity instantly diverts him from his previous purposes.

—William Hazlitt, *Characters of Shakespear's Plays* (London: Macmillan, 1817): pp. 65–68.

Friedrich Nietzsche on Hamlet's Dionysiac Traits

[Friedrich Nietzsche (1844–1900) was a German classical scholar, philosopher, and critic of culture. His important works include *Thus Spoke Zarathustra* (1883–92), *Beyond Good and Evil* (1886), and *On the Geneology of Morals* (1887). His book *The Birth of Tragedy* (1872), from which this extract is taken, contains his well-known Apollonian-Dionysian (rational-emotional) dichotomy. Here Nietzsche sees Hamlet as an example of the Dionysiac traits.]

For the rapture of the Dionysian state with its annihilation of the ordinary bounds and limits of existence contains, while it lasts, a *lethargic* element in which all personal experiences of the past become immersed. This chasm of oblivion separates the worlds of everyday reality and of Dionysian reality. But as soon as this everyday reality re-enters consciousness, it is experienced as such, with nausea: an ascetic, will-negating mood is the fruit of these states.

In this sense the Dionysian man resembles Hamlet: both have once looked truly into the essence of things, they have *gained knowledge,* and nausea inhibits action; for their action could not change anything in the eternal nature of things; they feel it to be ridiculous or humiliating that they should be asked to set right a world that is out of joint. Knowledge kills action; action requires the veils of illusion: that is the doctrine of Hamlet, not that cheap wisdom of Jack the Dreamer who reflects too much and, as it were, from an excess of possibilities does not get around to action. Not reflection, no—true knowledge, an insight into the horrible truth, outweighs any motive for action, both in Hamlet and in the Dionysian man.

—Friedrich Nietzsche, *The Birth of Tragedy* [1873], translated by Walter Kaufmann (New York: Vintage, 1967): 59–60.

Sigmund Freud on Hamlet's Deepest Impulses

[Sigmund Freud (1856–1939) is called the "father of psychoanalysis." Among his most important books that have been translated into English are *The Interpretation of Dreams* (1913) and *General Introduction to Psychoanalysis* (1920). Freud frequently devoted his attention to the study of literature from a psychoanalytic aspect. In this extract Freud discusses Hamlet's deepest impulses.]

Another of the great creations of tragic poetry, Shakespeare's *Hamlet,* has its roots in the same soil as *Oedipus Rex.* But the changed treatment of the same material reveals the whole difference in the mental life of these two widely separated epochs of civilization: the secular advance of repression in the emotional life of mankind. In the *Oedipus* the child's wishful phantasy that underlies it is brought into the open and realized as it would be in a dream. In *Hamlet* it remains repressed; and—just as in the case of a neurosis—we only learn of its existence from its inhibiting consequences. Strangely enough, the overwhelming effect produced by the more modern tragedy has turned out to be compatible with the fact that people have remained completely in the dark as to the hero's character. The play is built up on Hamlet's hesitations over fulfilling the task of revenge that is assigned to him; but its text offers no reasons or motives for these hesitations and an immense variety of attempts at interpreting them have failed to produce a result. According to the view which was originated by Goethe and is still the prevailing one to-day, Hamlet represents the type of man whose power of direct action is paralysed by an excessive development of his intellect. (He is 'sicklied o'er with the pale cast of thought'.) According to another view, the dramatist has tried to portray a pathologically irresolute character which might be classed as neurasthenic. The plot of the drama shows us, however, that Hamlet is far from being represented as a person incapable of taking any action. We see him doing so on two occasions: first in a sudden outburst of temper, when he runs his sword through the eavesdropper behind the arras, and secondly in a premeditated and even crafty fashion, when, with all the callousness of a Renaissance prince, he sends the two courtiers to the death that had been planned for himself. What is it, then, that inhibits him in fulfilling the task set him by his father's ghost? The answer, once again, is that it is the peculiar nature of the task. Hamlet is able to do anything—except take vengeance on the man who did away with his father and took that father's place with his mother, the man who shows him the repressed wishes of his own childhood realized. Thus the loathing which should drive him on to revenge is replaced in him by self-reproaches, by scruples of conscience, which remind him that he himself is literally no better than the sinner whom he is to punish. Here I have translated into conscious terms what was bound to remain unconscious in Hamlet's mind; and if anyone is inclined to call him a hysteric, I can only accept the fact as one is implied by my interpretation. The distaste for sexuality expressed by Hamlet in his conversation with Ophelia fits in very well with this: the same distaste which was destined to take possession of the poet's mind more and more during the years that followed, and which reached its extreme expression in *Timon of Athens.* For it can of course only be the poet's own mind which confronts us in Hamlet. I observe in a book on Shakespeare by Georg Brandes (1896) a statement that *Hamlet* was written immediately after the death of Shakespeare's father (in 1601), that is, under the immediate impact of his bereavement and, as we may well assume, while his childhood feelings about his father had been freshly revived. It is known, too, that Shakespeare's own son who died at any early age bore the name of 'Hamnet', which is identical with 'Hamlet'. Just as *Hamlet* deals with the relation of a son to his parents, so *Macbeth* (written at approximately the same period) is concerned with the subject of childlessness. But just as all neurotic symptoms, and, for that matter, dreams, are capable of being 'over-interpreted' and indeed need to be, if they are to be fully understood, so all genuinely creative writings are the product of more than a single motive and more than a single impulse in the poet's mind, and are open to more than a single interpretation. In what I have written I have only attempted to interpret the deepest layer of impulses in the mind of the creative writer.

—Sigmund Freud, *The Interpretations of Dreams* [1900], translated by James Stratchey et al. (London: Hogarth Press/Institute of Psycho-Analysis, 1953): pp. 264–266.

Harold C. Goddard on Hamlet's Hesitation

[Harold C. Goddard (1878–1950) was for many years head of the English department at Swarthmore College. He was the author of *Studies in New England Transcendentalism* (1906) and the editor of an edition of Ralph Waldo Emerson's essays (1926). One of the most important books on Shakespeare is Goddard's *The Meaning of Shakespeare,* published the year after his death. In this extract from that work, Goddard discusses why Hamlet hesitates.]

From the moment when Hamlet cries:

> The time is out of joint; O cursed spite,
> That ever I was born to set it right!

he becomes an example, unequalled in modern literature until Dostoevsky, of the Divided Man. "God and the Devil are fighting there, and the battlefield is the heart of man." That sentence of Dmitri Karamazov's expresses it, and because the infernal and celestial powers that are contending for the possession of Hamlet are so nearly in balance, the torture is prolonged and exquisite. He alternates between phases of anguished thought and feverish activity. Hence, as the one mood or the other is stressed, the opposing theories of his character. Hamlet is like a drunken man and you cannot determine whether he is going from his direction at any one moment. He lurches now to the right, now to the left. He staggers from passion to apathy, from daring to despair. To select his melancholy as the key to his conduct as Bradley does, is to offer the drunkard's fall as an explanation of his drunkenness. It is taking the effect for the cause, or fooling one's self, as Polonius did, with a word.

> Your noble son is mad:
> Mad call I it; for, to define true madness,
> What is't but to be nothing else but mad?
> But let that go.

Shakespeare is content with no such solution. To him melancholy is a symptom. He insists on getting under it to the cause that makes his melancholy characters melancholy. ⟨ . . . ⟩

Does the same diagnosis fit Hamlet? Obviously it does.

If these others were exceptional, Hamlet was as much one man among millions as Shakespeare was. He had precisely Shakespeare's interest in acting, playmaking, and drama. What if Shakespeare had turned from writing *Hamlets* and *King Lears* to go to war like Essex, or, like Hamlet, to run his rapier through an old man behind a curtain! What if Beethoven had fought with Napoleon instead of composing the *Eroica!* That, *mutatis mutandis,* is what Hamlet did. He did not know it. But his soul supplied plenty of evidence to that effect, if only he had had the power to read it.

We all hate in others the faults of which we are unaware in ourselves. And men of high endowment who are not doing what nature made them for exhibit this tendency in conspicuous degree.

> He that is giddy thinks the world turns round.

In that line Shakespeare caught in a striking image this propensity of the mind to project its unconscious contents. As early as *The Rape of Lucrece* he had written:

> Men's faults do seldom to themselves appear;
> Their own transgressions partially they smother:
> This guilt would seem death-worthy in thy brother,

and in the 121st sonnet:

> No, I am that I am, and they that level
> At my abuses reckon up their own:
> I may be straight, though they themselves be bevel;
> By their rank thoughts my deeds must not be shown.

Plainly Shakespeare had not merely observed this psychological effect in isolated instances. He understood it as a principle.

Now the moment we put Hamlet to this test we perceive that those around him become looking glasses in which, unknown to himself, his secret is reflected. (And this is particularly fitting in a work through which the symbol of the looking glass runs like a leitmotiv and whose central scene consists in the holding-up of a dramatic mirror in the form of a play within the play.)

To begin with, because Hamlet is trying to force himself to obey orders from his father to do something that his soul abhors, he hates with equal detestation those who issue orders and those who obey them, particularly fathers and children. This is plainly a main reason why Shakespeare allots to Polonius and his family so important a part in the play. Each of them seems expressly created to act as a mirror of some aspect of Hamlet. Polonius is a domestic tyrant wreaking on his son and his daughter revenge for his own spoiled life. His wife is dead, and except for one unrevealing allusion by her son, we are told nothing about her. Yet there she is! How she lived and what she died of we can readily imagine. As for Laertes, governments that want pugnacity in the younger generation should study his upbringing and act accordingly. But Ophelia is different. She is one more inexplicable daughter of her father (there are so many in Shakespeare). She is a mere child, just awakening into womanhood, and she unquestionably gives a true account of Hamlet's honorable "tenders of affection" to her. But Polonius fancies that Hamlet must be what he himself was at the same age ("I do not know") and in the scene in which we are first introduced to Ophelia we see first Laertes, aping his father, and then Polonius himself, pouring poison in her ear. Both brother and father fasten on her like insects on an opening rosebud.

Who plucks the bud before one leaf put forth?

It is like an echo of *Venus and Adonis* with the sexes reversed, the first step on the journey of which Ophelia's madness and death are the last. "Do not believe his vows." "I shall obey, my lord."

Who can doubt—what juxtapositions Shakespeare achieves!—that this scene was written to be placed just before the one between Hamlet and the Ghost? There another father pours poison of another kind into the ear of a son as innocent in his way as Polonius' daughter was in hers. The temptation this time is not to sensuality under the name of purity but to violence under the name of honor. It is Romeo's temptation as contrasted with Juliet's. The parallel is startling.

—Harold C. Goddard, *The Meaning of Shakespeare* (Chicago: University of Chicago Press, 1951): pp. 354–356.

Plot Summary of
Othello

Shakespeare's villainous Iago immediately reveals his hatred of Othello the Moor in the first scene of **Act I**. One of the reasons Iago hates Othello, the commander of the Venetian forces, is because Iago has been passed over in favor of Cassio for the post of lieutenant, and he has been given the less important post of ancient. He tells Roderigo, an admirer of the daughter of a Venetian senator named Brabantio, that under the cover of false loyalty he will advance toward his "peculiar end." Iago also persuades Roderigo to cause a scandal by informing Brabantio that his daughter, Desdomana, has eloped with Othello.

We get a first glimpse of the Moor, a magnanimous soldier, in scene two, as Iago warns Othello of Brabantio's rage. Cassio enters with a message of an urgent conference, regarding the expedition to Cyprus. As Othello exits and Iago begins to tell Cassio of Othello's secret marriage with Desdemona, he is interrupted by an enraged Brabantio, who accuses Othello of having won his daughter by sorcery. They all go to the Duke to settle the matter.

Scene three begins with the Duke ordering Othello to sail for Cyprus to fight the Turkish galleys. Brabantio accuses Othello, and the Moor admits that he has married Desdemona, but with her full consent and not by bewitching her. Upon her arrival, Desdemona confirms his words, and she asks for and receives permission to accompany her husband on his way to Cyprus. Othello prepares to depart at once and places Desdemona in the care of Iago. Because of his unrequited love for Desdemona, Roderigo threatens to drown himself. To this Iago replies that he will yet win her affections and tells him that the cuckolding of Othello will be the right revenge for both of them. In the soliloquy that follows, Iago reveals to the audience the evil within him.

There is a break in time between Act I and **Act II**. (The rest of the play's action takes place in only a few days.) Act II, scene one, the "storm scene," opens at a seaport in Cyprus, where it is revealed that the Turkish fleet has been destroyed by a tempest. The first ship to arrive is one with Iago, Emilia (Iago's wife and Desdemona's waiting woman), and Desdemona. Cassio welcomes them, and while they are waiting for Othello's ship to arrive, they talk lightly of women. Iago catches Cassio's slight touch of Desdemona's palm, and he realizes that he can ensnare Othello's lieutenant. Othello arrives at last and embraces Desdemona, addressing her with the words of piercing beauty that are full of shades of meaning:

> "O my fair warrior! . . .
> It gives me wonder great as my content

To see you here before me! O my soul's joy!
If after every tempest come such calms,
May the winds blow till they have waken'd death,
And let the labouring bark climb hills of seas
Olympus-high and duck again as low
As hell's from heaven. If it were now to die,
'Twere now to be most happy; for I fear
My soul hath here content so absolute
That not another comfort like this
Succeeds in unknown fate."

As soon as they all leave, Iago outlines his evil plan to Roderigo. He will provoke Cassio to a fight during the watch that night.

In a short scene (II, 2), Othello's herald proclaims a celebration of Othello's victory over the Turks and a feast in honor of his marriage.

In scene three, Iago gets Cassio, the watch commander, drunk and involves him in a brawl with Montano. When Othello arrives, Iago pretends to interfere. Othello discharges Cassio from service, after which Iago slyly advises Cassio to seek Desdemona's help in persuading Othello to restore his position. This advice will destroy Cassio, since Iago plans to insinuate to Othello that Cassio and Desdemona are having an affair. Iago is also determined to include Emilia in the plot.

Act III, scene one opens with Cassio and the musicians, who are prepared to play but are dismissed by the clown because they cannot play music "that may not be heard." When Cassio asks Emilia to arrange a meeting between him and Desdemona, he does precisely what Iago has schemed.

In the next scene, Othello sends Iago to his ships with letters and commands him to report back as soon as possible.

In scene three, considered by many the most dramatic in all of Shakespeare's works, Desdemona and Cassio are having a conversation in Emilia's presence. Othello approaches and observes Cassio slipping away; at this Iago takes advantage of the situation and insinuates that the meeting is suspicious. After Othello dismisses Desdemona (who urges him to recall Cassio), Iago asks Othello questions in such a manner that makes Othello doubtful about his wife's honesty. The seeds of jealousy have been sown. Many critics believe this scene is evidence that Othello succumbs too easily to jealousy's lure.

Emilia and Desdemona enter, and Othello, now full of horrible doubts, explains that his faint voice and strange behavior are due to a headache. Desdemona takes out her handkerchief (a gift from Othello) and wants to bind his forehead. Impatiently, Othello pushes away her hand, and the handkerchief drops. They leave together, but Emilia picks up the handkerchief. Iago snatches it from his wife's hand. It will help further his scheme, for in his own words: "Trifles light as air/Are to the jealous confirmations strong/As proofs of holy writ." Iago doesn't wait long to tell Othello, in rhetoric potent with sensual imagery, that he has overheard Cassio mutter in his sleep of Desdemona and that he saw him wipe his beard with her handkerchief. Othello, by now completely "eaten up with passion," vows revenge on both of them.

In Act III, scene four, Desdemona is still planning to intercede on Cassio's behalf. Othello's entrance interrupts her conversation with the clown. Othello demands the handkerchief she cannot provide. He recounts the magic qualities of the handkerchief and leaves abruptly as Cassio and Iago approach. Cassio is also joined by his mistress Bianca, to whom he gives the handkerchief he has found in his room, asking her to copy the embroidery for him.

In **Act IV**, we witness a particularly ghastly opening: Othello, goaded by Iago's continuing innuendoes, succumbs to a rage of jealousy in which he falls onto the floor in a trance that resembles an epileptic fit. Iago is delighted by Othello's complete loss of physical and mental control. Soon after this, in a scene staged by Iago, Othello overhears Cassio talking of Bianca to Iago, but he is under the impression that Cassio's words apply to Desdemona. Othello is now wholly convinced of Desdemona's infidelity. Iago's scheme proceeds successfully even when Bianca suddenly enters, because he is able to turn even her words to his advantage.

Desdemona enters with an emissary from the Duke of Venice, who bears a warrant recalling Othello to Venice and placing Cassio in charge of Cyprus. Desdemona's innocent reaction enrages Othello, who then strikes her, to the consternation of all. As Desdemona withdraws and Othello exits, Iago, alone with Lodovico, discredits Othello, saying that he has changed for the worse.

In scene two, Othello questions Emilia. She swears to Desdemona's innocence, but Othello cannot believe her. He sends Emilia for Desdemona, and when she enters, he vilifies and insults her with harsh words. Desdemona sends Emilia for Iago to ask him to explain her husband's conduct. Desdemona (embodied goodness) and Iago (pure evil) are never alone together, and this is the second time they are involved with what may be called dialogue (the first time is in the "storm scene"). Is Iago feigning compassion when he utters words like "I pray you be content" or "Go in, and weep not; all things shall be well"? Emilia suggests that some "rogue" who wants to advance in office has devised the slander. The two women leave and Roderigo arrives, complaining to Iago that despite his many gifts (sent through Iago) to Desdemona he hasn't heard from her (Iago has kept all the gifts). Iago again succeeds in soothing him and suggests to him that the only way to prevent Othello's departure from Cyprus with Desdemona is to kill Cassio.

Scene three shows Othello ordering Desdemona to prepare for bed. Full of foreboding, she sings the "Willow" song, which increases the scene's tension.

In **Act V**, scene one, Iago persuades Roderigo to attack Cassio. When Roderigo is wounded by Cassio, Iago, who has been standing near by, stabs

Cassio in the leg. Othello enters and hear Cassio's voice—"I am maim'd for ever! Help, ho! murder! murder!"—and he concludes that "honest Iago" has kept his word to kill Cassio. When Roderigo says, "O, villain that I am!" Othello mistakes his voice for Cassio's, and he is convinced that Cassio is admitting his guilt. He praises Iago's loyalty and leaves for Desdemona's chamber. In the scuffle that follows, Iago stabs Roderigo to death, ridding himself of a possible witness. A crowd gathers, including Bianca and Emilia. As the wounded Cassio is carried out in a chair, Iago, shifting attention from himself, tries to implicate Bianca. As the scene ends, Iago, aware that all his plotting has reached a climax, remarks: "This is the night/That either makes me or fordoes me quite."

In the final scene, Othello enters his wife's bedchamber and accuses her of infidelity. He smothers her, but still perceiving signs of life ("I would not have thee linger in thy pain"), he stabs her while saying, "So, so." At that moment Emilia enters with reports that it was Roderigo, and not Cassio, who has been murdered. Emilia hears a cry and approaches Desdemona with the question, "O who hath done this deed?" Desdemona responds with her last words: "Nobody—I myself." As Emilia attacks Othello, he tells her that he has learned about Desdemona's unfaithfulness from Iago. Emilia asks for help, and Iago appears with Montano and Gratiano, who bring the news that Brabantio has died of grief over his daughter's marriage. Othello mentions the handkerchief, and Emilia, understanding the scope of Iago's treachery, accuses Iago. He stabs her fatally; Othello, now in a state of clarity, manages to wound Iago before the Venetian gentlemen can seize the Moor. Emilia dies, and Othello, before stabbing himself, asks the gentlemen to:

> Speak of me as I am; nothing extenuate,
> Nor set down aught in malice. Then must you speak
> Of one that lov'd not wisely, but too well;
> Of one not easily jealous, but, being wrought,
> Perplexed in the extreme; of one whose hand,
> Like the base Indian, threw a pearl away
> Richer than all his tribe.

Lodovico promises that Iago will be tortured to death, and with a heavy heart, he himself will return to Venice to relate the story. ❁

List of Characters in
Othello

Othello is a Moorish soldier in the employ of the Venetian Senate. He "thinks men honest that but seem to be so." Othello secretly marries Desdemona and then easily succumbs to Iago's insinuations that his wife is not faithful to him. He suffocates Desdemona in a "brothel scene" and kills himself after realizing he has been deceived by "honest Iago."

Iago is Othello's ancient, or ensign, presented as a master of intrigue. Coleridge said that Iago exhibits "the motive-hunting of a motiveless malignity." A truly evil man, Iago murders Roderigo, after the latter fails to kill Cassio, and he kills his wife Emilia, after she betrays his secret. He does succeed in ruining Othello, but ultimately, as the Venetian commissioners decree, he will be put to death by torture.

Desdemona is Brabantio's daughter, who marries Othello without her father's consent. She is "chaste and heavenly true" (in Emilia's words) to Othello. Othello, though, strangles her, believing she has committed adultery with Cassio.

Cassio is Othello's newly appointed lieutenant. Iago manipulates Cassio in his plot against Othello, and succeeds in wounding, but not killing, Cassio. Cassio assumes Othello's post at the end of the play.

Emilia is Iago's wife and Desdemona's loyal waiting-woman. She unknowingly helps to bring about the tragedy when she gives Desdemona's handkerchief to Iago. She exposes her husband's villainy, and Iago kills her to silence her.

Roderigo is a gentleman in love with Desdemona, whom Iago uses in his revenge. Iago exploits his wealth as well. Roderigo is killed by Iago in the darkness after he attacks Cassio at Iago's urging.

Bianca is Cassio's mistress, whom Iago also uses in his plot against Othello.

Brabantio is a Venetian senator and Desdemona's father. He is outraged by her secret marriage to the Moor. At the end of the play, we hear that he has died of pure grief.

The Duke of Venice sends Othello to Cyprus, and he also acts as intermediary between Brabantio and Othello.

Lodovico is Brabantio's kinsman. He witnesses the final downfall of Othello.

Montano is the governor of Cyprus.

Gratiano is a relative of Desdemona. ✿

Critical Views on
Othello

SAMUEL JOHNSON ON IAGO'S CHARACTER

[Dr. Samuel Johnson (1709–1784), one of the outstanding British literary figures of the eighteenth century, was a poet, essayist, critic, journalist, and lexicographer. His *Dictionary of the English Language* (1755) was the first major English dictionary to use historical quotations. In 1765 he wrote a monograph, *Preface to His Edition of Shakespeare,* and in the same year he edited a landmark annotated edition of Shakespeare's works. In this short extract, Johnson analyzes Iago's character.]

The beauties of this play impress themselves so strongly upon the attention of the reader, that they can draw no aid from critical illustration. The fiery openness of Othello, magnanimous, artless, and credulous, boundless in his confidence, ardent in his affection, inflexible in his resolution, and obdurate in his revenge; the cool malignity of Iago, silent in his resentment, subtle in his designs, and studious at once of his interest and his vengeance; the soft simplicity of Desdemona, confident of merit, and conscious of innocence, her artless perseverance in her suit, and her slowness to suspect that she can be suspected, are such proofs of Shakespeare's skill in human nature, as, I suppose, it is vain to seek in any modern writer. The gradual progress which Iago makes in the Moor's conviction, and the circumstances which he employs to inflame him, are so artfully natural, that, though it will perhaps not be said of him as he says of himself, that he is "a man not easily jealous," yet we cannot but pity him when at last we find him "perplexed in the extreme."

There is always danger lest wickedness conjoined with abilities should steal upon esteem, though it misses of approbation; but the character of Iago is so conducted, that he is from the first scene to the last hated and despised.

—Samuel Johnson, *The Plays of William Shakespeare,* vol. 8 (London: J. & R. Tonson, 1765): p. 472.

WILLIAM HAZLITT ON OTHELLO'S MIND

[William Hazlitt (1778–1830) is an English writer best remembered for his essays. Among his many works are *Lectures on the English Poets* (1818), *Lectures on the English Comic Writers* (1819), and *Liber*

Amoris, in which he describes the suffering of a love affair that ended disastrously. In this extract taken from his *Characters of Shakespear's Plays* (1817), Hazlitt explores Othello's mind.]

The progressive preparation for the catastrophe is wonderfully managed from the Moor's first gallant recital of the story of his love, of "the spells and witchcraft he had used," from his unlooked-for and romantic success, the fond satisfaction with which he dotes on his own happiness, the unreserved tenderness of Desdemona and her innocent importunities in favour of Cassio, irritating the suspicions instilled into her husband's mind by the perfidy of Iago, and rankling there to poison, till he loses all command of himself, and his rage can only be appeased by blood. She is introduced, just before Iago begins to put his scheme in practice, pleading for Cassio with all the thoughtless gaiety of friendship and winning confidence in the love of Othello.

> "What! Michael Cassio?
> That came a wooing with you, and so many a time,
> When I have spoke of you dispraisingly,
> Hath ta'en your part, to have so much to do
> To bring him in?—Why this is not a boon:
> 'Tis as I should intreat you wear your gloves,
> Or feed on nourishing meats, or keep you warm;
> Or sue to you to do a peculiar profit
> To your person. Nay, when I have a suit,
> Wherein I mean to touch your love indeed,
> It shall be full of poise, and fearful to be granted."

Othello's confidence, at first only staggered by broken hints and insinuations, recovers itself at sight of Desdemona; and he exclaims

> "If she be false, O then Heav'n mocks itself:
> I'll not believe it."

But presently after, on brooding over his suspicions by himself, and yielding to his apprehensions of the worst, his smothered jealousy breaks out into open fury, and he returns to demand satisfaction of Iago like a wild beast stung with the envenomed shaft of the hunters. "Look where he comes," &c. In this state of exasperation and violence, after the first paroxysms of his grief and tenderness have had their vent in that passionate apostrophe, "I felt not Cassio's kisses on her lips," Iago, by false aspersions, and by presenting the most revolting images to his mind, easily turns the storm of passion from himself against Desdemona, and works him up into a trembling agony of doubt and fear, in which he abandons all his love and hopes in a breath.

> "Now do I see 'tis true. Look here, Iago,
> All my fond love thus do I blow to Heav'n. 'Tis gone.
> Arise black vengeance from the hollow hell;
> Yield up, O love, thy crown and hearted throne
> To tyrannous hate! Swell bosom with thy fraught;
> For 'tis of aspicks' tongues."

From this time, his raging thoughts "never look back, ne'er ebb to humble love," till his revenge is sure of its object, the painful regrets and involuntary recollections of past circumstances which cross his mind amidst the dim trances of passion, aggravating the sense of his wrongs, but not shaking his purpose. Once indeed, where Iago shews him Cassio with the handkerchief in his hand, and making sport (as he thinks) of his misfortunes, the intolerable bitterness of his feelings, the extreme sense of shame, makes him fall to praising her accomplishments and relapse into a momentary fit of weakness, "Yet, Oh the pity of it, Iago, the pity of it!" This returning fondness however only serves, as it is managed by Iago, to whet his revenge, and set his heart more against her. In his conversation with Desdemona, the persuasion of her guilt and the immediate proofs of her duplicity seem to irritate his resentment and aversion to her; but in the scene immediately preceding her death, the recollection of his love returns upon him in all its tenderness and force; and after her death, he all at once forgets his wrongs in the sudden and irreparable sense of his loss.

> "My wife! My wife! What wife? I have no wife.
> Oh insupportable! Oh heavy hour!"

This happens before he is assured of her innocence; but afterwards his remorse is as dreadful as his revenge has been, and yields only to fixed and death-like despair. His farewell speech, before he kills himself, in which he conveys his reasons to the senate for the murder of his wife, is equal to the first speech in which he gave them an account of his courtship of her, and "his whole course of love." Such an ending was alone worthy of such a commencement.

—William Hazlitt, *Characters of Shakespear's Plays* (London: Macmillan, 1817): pp. 29–31.

GEORGE BERNARD SHAW ON IAGO'S COMPLEX CHARACTER

[George Bernard Shaw (1856–1950) was an Irish dramatist and literary critic. Among his most famous plays are *The Devil's Disciple* (1897), *Caesar and Cleopatra* (1901), *Man and Superman* (1905), *Pygmalion* (1913; adapted into the popular musical and motion picture *My Fair Lady*), and *Saint Joan* (1923). Although he won the Nobel Prize for Literature in 1925, he refused the award. This extract is taken from Shaw's writings on the plays of Shakespeare. Here Shaw analyzes Iago's many-sided character.]

The character defies all consistency. Shakespeare, as usual, starts with a rough general notion of a certain type of individual, and then throws it over at the first temptation. Iago begins as a coarse blackguard, whose jovial bluntness passes as "honesty," and who is professionally a routine subaltern incapable of understanding why a mathematician gets promoted over his head. But the moment a stage effect can be made, or a fine speech brought off by making him refined, subtle and dignified, he is set talking like Hamlet, and becomes a godsend to students of the "problems" presented by our divine William's sham characters. Mr. [Franklin] McLeay does all that an actor can do with him. He follows Shakespeare faithfully on the rails and off them. He plays the jovial blackguard to Cassio and Roderigo and the philosopher and mentor to Othello just as the lines lead him, with perfect intelligibility and with so much point, distinction and fascination that the audience loads him with compliments, and the critics all make up their minds to declare that he shows the finest insight into the many-sided and complex character of the prince of villains.

—George Bernard Shaw, "Mainly About Shakespeare," *London Saturday Review,* (29 May 1897): p. 605.

A. C. Bradley on *Othello*'s Distinguishing Characteristics

[A. C. Bradley (1851–1935) was the leading British Shakespeare scholar of his time. He taught at the University of Liverpool, the University of Glasgow, and at Oxford University. In this extract, taken from his famous book *Shakespearean Tragedy* (1904), Bradley remarks on the most distinguished characteristics of *Othello.*]

What is the peculiarity of *Othello?* What is the distinctive impression that it leaves? Of all Shakespeare's tragedies, I would answer, not even excepting *King Lear, Othello* is the most painfully exciting and the most terrible. From the moment when the temptation of the hero begins, the reader's heart and mind are held in a vice, experiencing the extremes of pity and fear, sympathy and repulsion, sickening hope and dreadful expectation. Evil is displayed before him, not indeed with the profusion found in *King Lear,* but forming, as it were, the soul of a single character, and united with an intellectual superiority so great that he watches its advance fascinated and appalled. He sees it, in itself almost irresistible, aided at every step by fortunate accidents and the innocent mistakes of its victims. He seems to breathe an atmosphere as fateful as that of *King Lear,* but more confined and oppressive, the darkness not of night but of a close-shut murderous room. His imagination is excited to intense activity, but it is the activity of concentration rather than dilation.

I will not dwell now on aspects of the play which modify this impression, and I reserve for later discussion one of its principal sources, the character of Iago. But if we glance at some of its other sources, we shall find at the same time certain distinguishing characteristics of *Othello*.

(1) One of these has been already mentioned in our discussion of Shakespeare's technique. *Othello* is not only the most masterly of the tragedies in point of construction, but its method of construction is unusual. And this method, by which the conflict begins late, and advances without appreciable pause and with accelerating speed to the catastrophe, is a main cause of the painful tension just described. To this may be added that, after the conflict has begun, there is very little relief by way of the ridiculous. Henceforward at any rate Iago's humour never raises a smile. The clown is a poor one; we hardly attend to him and quickly forget him; I believe most readers of Shakespeare, if asked whether there is a clown in *Othello*, would answer No.

(2) In the second place, there is no subject more exciting than sexual jealousy rising to the pitch of passion; and there can hardly be any spectacle at once so engrossing and so painful as that of a great nature suffering the torment of this passion, and driven by it to a crime which is also a hideous blunder. Such a passion as ambition, however terrible its results, is not itself ignoble; if we separate it in thought from the conditions which make it guilty, it does not appear despicable; it is not a kind of suffering, its nature is active; and therefore we can watch its course without shrinking. But jealousy, and especially sexual jealousy, brings with it a sense of shame and humiliation. For this reason it is generally hidden; if we perceive it we ourselves are ashamed and turn our eyes away; and when it is not hidden it commonly stirs contempt as well as pity. Nor is this all. Such jealousy as Othello's converts human nature into chaos, and liberates the beast in man; and it does this in relation to one of the most intense and also the most ideal of human feelings. What spectacle can be more painful than that of this feeling turned into a tortured mixture of longing and loathing, the 'golden purity' of passion split by poison into fragments, the animal in man forcing itself into this consciousness in naked grossness, and he writhing before it but powerless to deny it entrance, gasping inarticulate images of pollution, and finding relief only in a bestial thirst for blood? This is what we have to witness in one who was indeed 'great of heart' and no less pure and tender than he was great. And this, with what it leads to, the blow to Desdemona, and the scene where she is treated as the inmate of a brothel, a scene far more painful than the murder scene, is another cause of the special effect of this tragedy.

(3) The mere mention of these scenes will remind us painfully of a third cause; and perhaps it is the most potent of all. I mean the suffering of Desdemona. This is, unless I mistake, the most nearly intolerable spectacle that Shakespeare offers us. For one thing, it is *mere* suffering; and, *ceteris paribus*, that is much worse to witness than suffering that issues in action. Desdemona

is helplessly passive. She can do nothing whatever. She cannot retaliate even in speech; no, not even in silent feeling. And the chief reason of her helplessness only makes the sight of her suffering more exquisitely painful. She is helpless because her nature is infinitely sweet and her love absolute. I would not challenge Mr Swinburne's statement that we *pity* Othello even more than Desdemona; but we watch Desdemona with more unmitigated distress. We are never wholly uninfluenced by the feeling that Othello is a man contending with another man; but Desdemona's suffering is like that of the most loving of dumb creatures tortured without cause by the being he adores.

(4) Turning from the hero and heroine to the third principal character, we observe (what has often been pointed out) that the action and catastrophe of *Othello* depend largely on intrigue. We must not say more than this. We must not call the play a tragedy of intrigue as distinguished from a tragedy of character. Iago's plot is Iago's character in action; and it is built on his knowledge of Othello's character, and could not otherwise have succeeded. Still it remains true that an elaborate plot was necessary to elicit the catastrophe; for Othello was no Leontes, and his was the last nature to engender such jealousy from itself. Accordingly Iago's intrigue occupies a position in the drama for which no parallel can be found in the other tragedies; the only approach, and that a distant one, being the intrigue of Edmund in the secondary plot of *King Lear*. Now in any novel or play, even if the persons rouse little interest and are never in serious danger, a skilfully worked intrigue will excite eager attention and suspense. And where, as in *Othello*, the persons inspire the keenest sympathy and antipathy, and life and death depend on the intrigue; it becomes the source of a tension in which pain almost overpowers pleasure. Nowhere else in Shakespeare do we hold our breath in such anxiety and for so long a time as in the later Acts of *Othello*.

(5) One result of the prominence of the element of intrigue is that *Othello* is less unlike a story of private life than any other of the great tragedies. And this impression is strengthened in further ways. In the other great tragedies the action is placed in a distant period, so that its general significance is perceived through a thin veil which separates the persons from ourselves and our own world. But *Othello* is a drama of modern life; when it first appeared it was a drama almost of contemporary life, for the date of the Turkish attack on Cyprus is 1570. The characters come close to us, and the application of the drama to ourselves (if the phrase may be pardoned) is more immediate than it can be in *Hamlet* or *Lear*. Besides this, their fortunes affect us as those of private individuals more than is possible in any of the later tragedies with the exception of *Timon*. I have not forgotten the Senate, nor Othello's position, nor his service to the State; but his deed and his death have not that influence on the interests of a nation or an empire which serves to idealize, and to remove far from our own sphere, the stories of Hamlet and Macbeth, of Coriolanus and Antony. Indeed he is already superseded at Cyprus when his fate

is consummated, and as we leave him no vision rises on us, as in other tragedies, of peace descending on a distracted land.

—A. C. Bradley, *Shakespearean Tragedy* (London: Macmillan, 1904): pp. 168–171.

WILLIAM EMPSON ON GOOD AND EVIL IN *OTHELLO*

[Sir William Empson (1906–1984) was a British poet and critic remembered for his immense influence on twentieth-century literary criticism and for his metaphysical poetry. *Seven Types of Ambiguity* (1930) is essentially a close examination of poetic texts. He applied his critical method to longer texts in *Some Versions of Pastoral* (1935) and in *The Structure of Complex Words* (1951). He taught English literature at the University of Tokyo, Peking National University of China, and at Sheffield University. In this extract, Empson discusses honor, honesty, good, and evil in *Othello*.]

The play has made Othello the personification of honour; if honour does not survive some test of the idea nor could Othello. And to him *honest* is "honourable," from which it was derived; a test of one is a test of the other. Outlive Desdemona's chastity, which he now admits, outlive Desdemona herself, the personification of chastity (lying again, as he insisted, with her last breath), outlive decent behaviour in, public respect for, self-respect in, Othello—all these are honour, not honesty; there is no question whether Othello outlives them. But they are not tests of an idea; what has been tested is a special sense of *honest*. Iago has been the personification of honesty, not merely to Othello but to his world; why should honour, the father of the word, live on and talk out itself; honesty, that obscure bundle of assumptions, the play has destroyed. I can see no other way to explain the force of the question here.

There is very little for anybody to add to A. C. Bradley's magnificent analysis, but one can maintain that Shakespeare, and the audience he had, and the audience he wanted, saw the thing in rather different proportions. Many of the audience were old soldiers disbanded without pension; they would dislike Cassio as the new type of officer, the boy who can displace men of experience merely because he knows enough mathematics to work the new guns. The play plays into their hands by making Cassio a young fool who can't keep his mistress in order and can't drink. Iago gets a long start at the beginning of the play, where he is enchantingly amusing and may be in the right. I am not trying to deny that by the end of the first act he is obviously the villain, and that by the end of the play we are meant to feel the mystery of his life as Othello did—

> Will you, I pray, demand that demi-devil
> Why he hath thus ensnared my soul and body?

Shakespeare can now speak his mind about Iago through the conventional final speech by the highest in rank:

> O Spartan dog,
> More fell than anguish, hunger, or the sea.

Verbal analysis is not going to weaken the main shape of the thing. But even in this resounding condemnation the *dog* is not simple. The typical Shakespearean dogmen are Apemantus and Thersites (called "dog" by Homer), malign underdogs, snarling critics, who yet are satisfactory as clowns and carry something of the claim of the disappointed idealist; on the other hand, if there is an obscure prophecy in the treatment of *honest*, surely the "honest dog" of the Restoration may cast something of his shadow before. Wyndham Lewis' interesting treatment of Iago as "fox" leaves out both these dogs, though the dog is more relevant than the fox on his analogy of tragedy to bull-baiting; indeed the clash of the two dogs goes to the root of Iago. But the *dog* symbolism is a mere incident, like that of *fool;* the thought is carried on *honest,* and I throw in the others only not to over-simplify the thing. Nor are they used to keep Iago from being a simple villain; the point is that more force was needed to make Shakespeare's audience hate Iago than to make the obviously intolerable Macbeth into a tragic hero.

There seems a linguistic difference between what Shakespeare meant by Iago and what the nineteenth century critics saw in him. They took him as an abstract term "Evil"; he is a critique on an unconscious pun. This is seen more clearly in their own personification of their abstract word; e.g. *The Turn of The Screw* and *Dr. Jekyll and Mr. Hyde.* Henry James got a great triumph over some critics who said his villains were sexual perverts (if the story meant anything they could hardly be anything else). He said "Ah, you have been letting yourself have fancies about Evil; I kept it right out of my mind." That indeed is what the story is about. Stevenson rightly made clear that *Dr. Jekyll* is about hypocrisy. You can only consider Evil as all things that destroy the good life; this has no unity; for instance, Hyde could not be both the miser and the spendthrift and whichever he was would destroy Jekyll without further accident. Evil here is merely the daydream of a respectable man, and only left vague so that respectable readers may equate it unshocked to their own daydreams. Iago may not be a "personality," but he is better than these; he is a product of a more actual interest in a word.

—William Empson, "The Best Policy," *Life and Letters To-day* 14, no. 4 (Summer 1936): pp. 44–45.

Harold C. Goddard on *Othello*'s Inaudible Music

[Harold C. Goddard (1878–1950) was for many years head of the English department at Swarthmore College. He was the author of *Studies in New England Transcendentalism* (1906) and the editor of an edition of Ralph Waldo Emerson's essays (1926). One of the most important books on Shakespeare is Goddard's *The Meaning of Shakespeare,* published the year after his death. In this extract, Goddard discusses the inaudible music and its meaning in *Othello.*]

If readers of *Othello* were asked to select the most supererogatory passage in the play, they would probably be unanimous, unless some forgot its very existence, in picking the opening of Act III where Cassio comes in with some musicians who are prepared to play but are peremptorily dismissed by the Clown (for there *is* a clown in *Othello*):

CLOWN: Then put up your pipes in your bag, for I'll away. Go; vanish into air, away! (*Exeunt Musicians*)

This brief overture to what is admittedly one of the greatest acts Shakespeare ever wrote is a tolerably obvious allegory of that sudden interruption of the music of Othello's love which is to be the subject of the act—a fact that in itself justifies us, apart from its very inconsequentiality, in searching it for other clues.

The passage emphasizes the fact that it is upon wind instruments that the musicians are prepared to play, and the Clown himself plays on that idea when he tells them to "vanish into air." Vanish into your proper element, he might have said. The other thing stressed is the idea of inaudible music:

CLOWN: But, masters, here's money for you: and the general so likes your music, that he desires you, for love's sake, to make no more noise with it.

FIRST MUS.:   Well, sir, we will not.

CLOWN: If you have any music that may not be heard, to't again: but, as they say, to hear music the general does not greatly care.

FIRST MUS.:   We have none such, sir.

This sounds like the idlest fooling, and on the surface it is just that. But when we remember Keats's

> Heard melodies are sweet, but those unheard
> Are sweeter; therefore, ye soft pipes, play on;
> Not to the sensual ear, but, more endear'd,
> Pipe to the spirit ditties of no tone,

we see that, so far from mere fooling, this idea of inaudible music is the idea of poetry itself brought down by the Clown to the level of burlesque and parody. The quintessence of a poem is precisely its music that may not be heard. May not, notice, not cannot.

Where, audible or inaudible, is there music in Othello? Where, especially, if anywhere, is there wind music?

We think immediately of the storm off Cyprus. There the gale roared until Montano cried, "The wind hath spoke aloud." There it tossed water on the very stars, bringing a chaos of the elements that forecasts the chaos that "is come again" in Othello's soul when Iago loosens the moral hurricane that parts the Moor from his wife more violently than ever the physical tempest did. The Turks go down in the first storm. Turk-Iago goes down in the second one. Othello and Desdemona were parted by the first storm, but were reunited after it. They were parted by the second one. Was there a Second Cyprus?

If Shakespeare carries his symbolism through with Iago, is it inconceivable that he may have done the same with Desdemona and Othello? Here, if anywhere, it would be natural to seek the poetry of this poem, the music in this play that may not be heard.

A scientist gets his hypothesis from he does not always know where. He subjects it to the test of facts, and accepts it or rejects it accordingly. So it should be with the interpretation of a work of literary art. Where a suggested reading comes from is not the important question. The important question is whether it can pass the test of the text. If not, however alluring, it must be dismissed.

—Harold C. Goddard, *The Meaning of Shakespeare* (Chicago: University of Chicago Press, 1951): pp. 99–101.

W. H. Auden on Iago as a Practical Joker

[W. H. Auden (1907–1973) was one of the leading twentieth-century British poets as well as an important critic. Most of his verse dramas were written with Christopher Isherwood. This extract is taken from his critical work collected in *The Dyer's Hand and Other Essays* (1962). Here, Auden regards Iago as a practical joker.]

Any consideration of the Tragedy of Othello must be primarily occupied, not with its official hero but with its villain. I cannot think of any other play in which only one character performs personal actions—all the *deeds* are Iago's—and all the others without exception only exhibit behavior. In marrying each other, Othello and Desdemona have performed a deed, but this took place before the play begins. Nor can I think of another play in which the villain is so completely triumphant: everything Iago sets out to do, he accomplishes—(among his goals, I include his self-destruction). Even Cassio, who survives, is maimed for life.

If *Othello* is a tragedy—and one certainly cannot call it a comedy—it is tragic in a peculiar way. In most tragedies the fall of the hero from glory to misery and death is the work, either of the gods, or of his own freely chosen acts, or, more commonly, a mixture of both. But the fall of Othello is the work of another human being; nothing he says or does originates with himself. In consequence we feel pity for him but no respect; our aesthetic respect is reserved for Iago.

Iago is a wicked man. The wicked man, the stage villain, as a subject of serious dramatic interest does not, so far as I know, appear in the drama of Western Europe before the Elizabethans. In the mystery plays, the wicked characters, like Satan or Herod, are treated comically, but the theme of the triumphant villain cannot be treated comically because the suffering he inflicts is real.

A distinction must be made between the villainous character—figures like Don John in *Much Ado,* Richard III, Edmund in *Lear,* Iachimo in *Cymbeline*—and the merely criminal character—figures like Duke Antonio in *The Tempest,* Angelo in *Measure for Measure,* Macbeth or Claudius in *Hamlet.* The criminal is a person who finds himself in a situation where he is tempted to break the law and succumbs to the temptation: he ought, of course, to have resisted the temptation, but everybody, both on stage and in the audience, must admit that, had they been placed in the same situation, they, too, would have been tempted. The opportunities are exceptional—Prospero, immersed in his books, has left the government of Milan to his brother, Angelo is in a position of absolute authority, Claudius is the Queen's lover, Macbeth is egged on by prophecies and heaven-sent opportunities, but the desire for a dukedom or a crown or a chaste and beautiful girl are desires which all can imagine themselves feeling. ⟨ . . . ⟩

All practical jokes, friendly, harmless or malevolent, involve deception, but not all deceptions are practical jokes. The two men digging up the street, for example, might have been two burglars who wished to recover some swag which they knew to be buried there. But, in that case, having found what they were looking for, they would have departed quietly and never been heard of again, whereas, if they are practical jokers, they must reveal afterwards what they have done or the joke will be lost. The practical joker must not only deceive but also, when he has succeeded, unmask and reveal the truth to his victims. The satisfaction of the practical joker is the look of astonishment on the faces of others when they learn that all the time they were convinced that they were thinking and acting on their own initiative, they were actually the puppets of another's will. Thus, though his jokes may be harmless in themselves and extremely funny, there is something slightly sinister about every practical joker, for they betray him as someone who likes to play God behind the scenes. Unlike the ordinary ambitious man who strives for a dominant position in public and enjoys giving orders and seeing others obey them, the practical joker desires to makes others obey him without being aware of his existence until the moment of this theophany when he says: "Behold the God whose puppets you have been and behold, he does not look like a god but is a human being just like yourselves." The success of a practical joker depends upon his accurate estimate of the weaknesses of others, their ignorances, their social reflexes, their unquestioned presuppositions, their obsessive desires, and even the most harmless practical joke is an expression of the joker's contempt for those he deceives.

But, in most cases, behind the joker's contempt for others lies something else, a feeling of self-insufficiency, of a self lacking in authentic feelings and desires of its own. The normal human being may have a fantastic notion of himself, but he believes in it; he thinks he knows who he is and what he wants so that he demands recognition by others of the value he puts upon himself and must inform others of what he desires if they are to satisfy them.

But the self of the practical joker is unrelated to his joke. He manipulates others but, when he finally reveals his identity, his victims learn nothing about his nature, only something about their own; they know how it was possible for them to be deceived but only why he chose to deceive them. The only answer that any practical joker can give to the question: "Why did you do this?" is Iago's: "Demand me nothing. What you know, you know."

In fooling others, it cannot be said that the practical joker satisfies any concrete desire of his nature; he has only demonstrated the weaknesses of others and all he can now do, once he has revealed his existence, is to bow and retire from the stage. He is only related to others, that is, so long as they are unaware of his existence, once they are made aware of it, he cannot fool them again, and the relation is broken off.

The practical joker despises his victims, but at the same time he envies them because their desires, however childish and mistaken, are real to them, whereas he has no desire which he can call his own. His goal, to make game of others, makes his existence absolutely dependent upon theirs; when he is alone, he is a nullity. Iago's self-description, *I am not what I am*, is correct and the negation of the Divine *I am that I am*. If the word motive is given its normal meaning of a positive purpose of the self like sex, money, glory, etc., then the practical joker is without motive. Yet the professional practical joker is certainly driven, like a gambler, to his activity, but the drive is negative, a fear of lacking a concrete self, or being nobody. In any practical joker to whom playing such jokes is a passion, there is always an element of malice, a projection of his self-hatred onto others, and in the ultimate case of the absolute practical joker, this is projected onto all created things. ⟨ . . . ⟩

The other method is to play on the fears and desires of which you are aware and they are not until they enslave themselves. In this case, concealment of your real intention is not only possible but essential for, if people know they are being played upon, they will not believe what you say or do what you suggest. An advertisement based on snob appeal, for example, can only succeed with people who are unaware that they are snobs and that their snobbish feelings are being appealed to and to whom, therefore, your advertisement seems as honest as Iago seems to Othello.

Iago's treatment of Othello conforms to Bacon's definition of scientific enquiry as putting Nature to the Question. If a member of the audience were to interrupt the play and ask him: "What are you doing?" could not Iago answer with a boyish giggle, "Nothing. I'm only trying to find out what Othello is really like"? And we must admit that his experiment is highly successful. By the end of the play he does know the scientific truth about the object to which he has reduced Othello. That is what makes his parting shot, "What you know, you know," so terrifying for, by then, Othello has become a thing, incapable of knowing anything.

And why shouldn't Iago do this? After all, he has certainly acquired knowledge. What makes it impossible for us to condemn him self-righteously is that, in our culture, we have all accepted the notion that the right to know is absolute and unlimited. The gossip column is one side of the medal; the cobalt bomb the other. We are quite prepared to admit that, while food and sex are good in themselves, an uncontrolled pursuit of either is not, but it is difficult for us to believe that intellectual curiosity is a desire like any other, and to realize the correct knowledge and truth are not identical. To apply a categorical imperative to knowing, so that, instead of asking, "What can I know?" we ask, "What, at this moment, am I meant to know?"—to entertain the possibility that the only knowledge which can be true for us is the knowledge we can live up to—that seems to all of us crazy and almost immoral. But, in that case, who are we to say to Iago—"No, you mustn't."

—W. H. Auden, *The Dyer's Hand and Other Essays* (New York: Random House, 1962): pp. 246–72.

HAROLD BLOOM ON IAGO'S MANIPULATIONS

[Harold Bloom, the editor of this series, is Sterling Professor of the Humanities at Yale University and Berg Professor of English at New York University. He is the author of more than 20 books and the editor of over 40 anthologies of both literature and literary criticism. His latest book, *Shakespeare: the Invention of the Human,* was published in November 1998. In this extract, taken from the introduction to a critical work on *Iago* in the Chelsea House series, MODERN LITERARY CHARACTERS, Bloom explores Iago's manipulations.]

For me, the Shakespearean question to ask concerning Iago is: how does he change in the course of the drama? Unlike Macbeth, Iago does not progressively lose control of his own imagination. What makes *The Tragedy of Othello, the Moor of Venice* so harrowing a work is the total triumph of Iago, until he is brought down so unexpectedly by his wife's outrage at the victimage of Desdemona. Iago's changes, until Emilia's courage ends him, are marches of triumphalism, in which he perpetually astonishes himself by his own manipulative genius. Yet that is only part of the story, the emergence of Iago as appreciative dramatic critic of his own power in composition. There is another side to this triumphalism, and that is the extent to which Iago, as great improviser, traps himself also in his own web. More successful at manipulating Othello than he could have imagined, he is forced into a situation where he must prove Othello's love a whore, or himself be slain by Othello. His extraordinary status as pure negation gives at once unlimited intellect, an overwhelming sense of nothingness, and a primal ambivalence towards Othello's massive, ontological presence that drives him beyond even his worked-out plottings. In this he differs from Edmund, who keeps to plan until the bodies of Goneril and Regan are brought in. Iago changes with each fresh confrontation, whether with Othello or with Desdemona, until he enters the final changelessness of his silence, prompted by outrage at Emilia's courageous devotion to the murdered and slandered Desdemona.

Iago tells us that he is nothing if not critical, and that he has never found a man that knew how to love himself. We can apply both these self-judgments to one of the most extraordinary moments in the play, when Emilia has given

Iago the handkerchief and then been sent away by him (Act III, scene iii, lines 318–29). Alone on stage, Iago exults at his own mastery, and then is moved to a marvelous and horrible aesthetic apprehension of the ruined Othello, the fallen god of honorable war, and now Iago's masterpiece:

> I will in Cassio's lodging lose this napkin
> And let him find it. Trifles light as air
> Are to the jealous confirmations strong
> As proofs of Holy Writ. This may do something.
> The Moor already changes with my poison:
> Dangerous conceits are in their natures poisons,
> Which at the first are scarce found to distaste,
> But, with a little, act upon the blood,
> Burn like the mines of sulfur. I did say so.
> *Enter Othello.*
> Look where he comes! No poppy nor mandragora,
> Nor all the drowsy syrups of the world,
> Shall ever medicine thee to that sweet sleep
> Which thou owedst yesterday.

We shudder and yet, for this great moment, we *are* Iago, or perhaps Iago is already John Keats and Walter Pater, particularly as he rolls out those sensuous negatives: "Not poppy nor mandragora, / Nor all the drowsy syrups of the world . . . " For he is nothing if not critical, and he chants an appreciation of his own poisonous art, relishing each syllable of "poppy" and "mandragora" and "drowsy syrups" and "sweet sleep." Aesthetic awareness in our modern sense, the poetic self-consciousness of Keats and Pater and the sublime Oscar Wilde, is invented by Iago in this grand negative moment. The excited apprehension of: "This may do something" leads to the conscious pride of "I did say so," as Iago hymns the power of his own "dangerous conceits." It is only a step from this to that still more dangerous prevalence of the murderous imagination that will triumph even more sublimely in the strongest of all Shakespearean negations, Macbeth.

—Harold Bloom, Introduction to *Iago* (New York: Chelsea House Publishers, 1992): pp. 3–5.

Plot Summary of
King Lear

In the opening scene of **Act I** King Lear behaves as the very embodiment of royal authority. He wants to divide his kingdom among his three daughters, Goneril, Regan, and Cordelia. He is administering a love-test: his daughter's statement of love for him will determine the portion of the kingdom she will receive. The two oldest, Goneril, wife of the Duke of Albany, and Regan, wife of the Duke of Cornwall, lavishly declare their love, and the old King is pleased. This makes self-willed Cordelia's answer, "nothing," all the more shocking. The King, in a rage, disinherits her. When the Earl of Kent protests, Lear banishes him. While the Duke of Burgundy (one of Cordelia's suitors) refuses to wed the disinherited bride, the King of France recognizes Cordelia's character and, honoring her for her virtues, takes her as his wife.

In scene two, the subplot that parallels the main plot is introduced. The scene takes place in the Earl of Gloucester's castle. Edmund, the bastard son of the earl of Gloucester, reveals his nature in his opening soliloquy. He intends to trick his father by fabricating a villainous letter in order to deprive his brother Edgar of his inheritance. Gloucester believes Edmund's fabrication and wrongs his faithful son, Edgar, in the same way that Lear wrongs Cordelia.

In scene three, Goneril and Oswald, her steward, discuss the conduct of King Lear and his knights, which increasingly displeases her. She asks Oswald to be negligent to the King so that she will have an excuse to send him earlier to Regan.

In scene four, King Lear realizes the mistake he's made by giving away his kingdom. The faithful Kent, disguised, returns to serve his old master. The Fool, who has a complex intimacy with Lear, is introduced for the first time (he will disappear silently after the sixth scene of Act III). His comments (tender and full of common sense) not only serve as a constant reminder of Lear's plight but also as a reminder of Cordelia. Purposely humiliating him by reducing the number of his retinue, Goneril forces King Lear to depart for Regan's.

In the brief fifth scene of Act I, King Lear prepares to leave, hoping that Regan will treat him with kindness. The Fool remarks upon his folly.

In **Act II,** scene one, Edmund confirms his father's conviction that Edgar is a villain. He also persuades Edgar to flee and escape his father's anger. Edmund wounds himself and later tells his father that he has been wounded while he and Edgar fought over Gloucester's honor. Regan and the Duke of

Cornwall arrive in order to avoid meeting with Lear at their home. Also, Regan suggests that Edgar consorts with Lear's "riotous knights."

In scene two, Kent, upon his arrival at Gloucester's castle, is put into the stocks by Regan and her husband for offending Oswald. Gloucester expresses his sorrow about Kent, but leaves him in the stocks. In scene three, we find Edgar in a wood disguising himself as "Poor Tom."

In scene four, Lear returns to Gloucester's castle after he has found nobody at home at Regan's. He becomes enraged at the sight of Kent in stocks and cannot believe that Regan and Cornwall have done it. Asking for an explanation, he finds only disrespect, since his daughter doesn't even want to see him. The situation becomes unbearable to him. Finally, when Regan appears with Cornwall and Kent is freed, Lear tells them of Goneril's mistreatment. At this moment, Goneril also arrives and both sisters agree that the King must now obey their rules. Beside himself with rage and humiliation, King Lear leaves the castle, fleeing into the stormy night with the words: "No, I'll not weep./I have full cause of weeping; but this heart/ Shall break into a hundred thousand flaws/Or ere I'll weep. O fool, I shall go mad!"

Act III, scene one, takes place amid the storm on an open heath. Kent discusses with a gentleman the ravings of the King. He also informs him that a secret strife is going on between Albany and Cornwall, and that the King of France is about to invade England. Kent sends the man to Dover to seek out Cordelia.

In scene two, King Lear, on another part of the heath, rages against the storm. Only the Fool follows him. Kent later finds the King and persuades him to go to a nearby hovel.

In the third scene, Gloucester confides to Edmund that he has received a secret letter telling of the French forces that want to help the King. He is resolute to join them, even at the risk of his life. Deceitful Edmund resolves to tell everything to Cornwall.

In scene four, King Lear and his Fool find Edgar still disguised as a beggar in the hovel. Gloucester arrives with a torch, risking the fury of Goneril and Regan, to take Lear to a better shelter. Gloucester, however, fails to recognize his son. He speaks to Kent of the evil he believes Edgar has done.

In the fifth scene, Edmund betrays his father to Cornwall, who vows to avenge himself and promises to award Edmund with the title Earl of Gloucester.

In the meantime (scene six) Gloucester leaves Lear, Kent, the Fool, and Edgar in a building outside his castle, then returns immediately to warn that the King's life is in danger and that he must flee to Dover.

In Act III, scene seven, Cornwall sends Edmund and Goneril to Albany with the news about the French army. Gloucester is brought in and accused of treachery. Cornwall and Regan confront him. Cornwall gouges out Gloucester's eyes; a servant protests and wounds Cornwall. Regan takes a sword and runs it through the servant from behind. When Gloucester asks for his son Edmund, Regan tells him that it was Edmund who had plotted against him. The horrible scene closes as she thrusts Gloucester out of the castle, saying "let him smell his way to Dover."

In **Act IV,** scene one, Poor Tom (Edgar) encounters his blind father, led by an old man. Gloucester confesses his mistaken wrath to the old man. He utters the unforgettable lines: "As flies to wanton boys are we to th' gods—/ They kill us for their sport." Without revealing himself, Edgar becomes his father's guide to Dover.

In scene two, Goneril arrives with Edmund to see Albany. Oswald reports that Albany seems greatly changed; in Oswald's words: "What most he should dislike seems pleasant to him; What like, offensive." Goneril kisses Edmund and sends him back to Regan. Albany denounces his wife for her cruelty; a messenger comes in with news of the death of Cornwall and the blinding of Gloucester. Goneril fears that Regan, now a widow, is a rival for Edmund's love.

In scene three, Kent reaches the French camp and learns that the King of France has suddenly returned to France. However, Cordelia stays with the troops. Kent tells the gentleman that Lear is in Dover, but he is ashamed to see Cordelia.

In scene four, Cordelia learns of Lear's condition and sends a soldier to find him. The British army approaches, and Cordelia insists on meeting them.

In scene five, Regan, jealous of her sister, prevents Oswald from delivering the letter from Goneril to Edmund. She sends Oswald back to her sister with the news that since Cornwall is dead, she wants to marry Edmund.

In the famous cliff scene stage, managed by Edgar (scene six), he pretends to lead Gloucester to a cliff near Dover and plays a trick on his father. Gloucester wants to commit suicide and jumps; Edgar, pretending to be another person, persuades Gloucester that he has been miraculously saved. Gloucester vows to bear his affliction till the end. Critics disagree as to whether this scene is tragic, grotesque, or farcical.

At this point, Lear enters, garlanded with wild flowers, railing against the corruption and hypocrisy of humanity. When Lear finally recognizes Gloucester, he cries, "When we are born, we cry that we are come/ To this great stage of fools." One of Cordelia's gentlemen arrives to take Lear to Cordelia, but Lear runs away. Oswald appears and attempts to kill Gloucester, but Edgar slays Oswald instead. Edgar finds Goneril's letter to Edmund in which she urges Edmund to kill Albany and marry her.

In Act IV, scene seven, Cordelia meets with Kent, who is still disguised. Lear is in bed in the next room. Cordelia embraces him and he begs for her forgiveness. The act ends with the account of the British army's approach, as the French prepare to confront Cornwall's army led by Edmund.

Act V opens in the British camp, where Edmund and Regan prepare for the battle. When Goneril and Albany arrive, Goneril admits that she would rather lose the battle than lose Edmund to Regan, so consumed is she with jealousy. Edgar, this time disguised as a peasant, gives Albany the letter that reveals Goneril's intentions.

Scene two shows Cordelia's army crossing the stage. Edgar leaves Gloucester under a tree, only to arrive a few moments later with the report that King Lear and Cordelia have been captured. Gloucester memorably says: "A man may rot even here," to which Edgar's response is "Men must endure/Their going hence, even as their coming hither: Ripeness is all." Critics have often wondered: does Shakespeare himself speak through these lines?

In the final scene Edmund enters with Cordelia and Lear. He sends them off to prison. Albany enters with Goneril and Regan and asks for the captives. Regan and Goneril begin to quarrel over Edmund, but Albany interrupts them, accusing Edmund of treason and challenging him to fight. Feeling unwell, Regan leaves the stage. At this point Edgar arrives, disguised in armor, and fights with Edmund. Edmund falls, mortally wounded. Goneril learns from Albany that he knows of her plot against him, and she leaves. Edgar reveals himself. Gloucester is so overcome with joy that he dies. The messenger enters with a bloody knife: Regan was poisoned by Goneril, and Goneril has stabbed herself to death. Albany orders the bodies of Goneril and Regan to be brought in. At the sight of their bodies, the dying Edmund comments: "Yet Edmund was belov'd," and then, "despite his own nature," he admits he has ordered Cordelia to be hanged. An officer rushes to try to save her. However, it is too late.

The entry of Lear with Cordelia in his arms has been much debated. Whatever Lear sees or imagines he sees, whether he thinks her alive or dead, Cordelia will come no more. "Do you see this? Look on her. Look, her lips./Look there, look there!" As he dies Kent cries: "Break heart, I prithee break." The weight of the play's sad ending is left for Edgar to bear.

The play makes absolutely clear, as Rosalie Colie observed, that virtue is hardly its own reward—and it provides us with no substitute reward, nor hope either. In its unnerving intensity, ambiguity, and multiple perspectives, *King Lear* remains a mystery too deep for critical analysis. ❀

List of Characters in
King Lear

King Lear is ruler of Britain ("every inch a king") and the person "more sinned against than sinning." He is patriarchal figure whose misjudgment of his daughters brings him to his emotional and physical downfall.

Goneril is the eldest daughter of King Lear, wife to the Duke of Albany. In the love-test she tells the old king exactly what he wants to hear and is awarded a part of his kingdom. She betrays him in cooperation with her sister Regan, whom she poisons later in the play because of their jealous quarrel over Edmund. After Edmund is wounded, she stabs herself. Goneril is presented as pitiless in her cruelty.

Regan is the second daughter of King Lear and wife to the Duke of Cornwall. In Act I, scene one, she skillfully flatters her father and gets part of his kingdom. When her husband blinds Gloucester, she eggs him on. She is poisoned by Goneril.

Cordelia (the name's meaning is "ideal heart," since "cor" means "heart" in Greek and "delia" is an anagram of "ideal") is the youngest and best-loved daughter of King Lear. She plays a relatively small part in the play, but we feel her presence even in her absence. In the love-test, she shows disobedience to her father by answering: " I love your Majesty/According to my bond; no more nor less." Lear is enraged and disinherits her. The King of France marries her without a dowry. Dr. Johnson found Cordelia's death in the last scene of the play so unbearable that he couldn't "endure to read it again."

The Duke of Albany is Goneril's husband. She scorns him for his "milky gentleness." Later in the play he turns to rage when he discovers her machinations.

The Duke of Cornwall is Regan's husband. He has Kent put in the stocks, leaves Lear out on the heath in the storm, and gouges out Gloucester's eyes and crushes them underfoot. During this last incident, one of the servants attacks him and mortally wounds him.

The Earl of Gloucester is the father of Edgar and the illegitimate Edmund. He is easily deceived by Edmund against Edgar. He sees clearly only after he loses his sight. When Edgar, before a duel with Edmund, asks his father for his blessing and reveals who he really is, Gloucester dies ("'Twixt two extremes of passion, joy and grief,/Burst smilingly").

The Earl of Kent is a faithful follower of King Lear. When he rebukes Lear because of his treatment of Cordelia, the King banishes him. Disguised as a serving man, he continues to serve Lear. He is often seen as "the quintessence of the good servant" and a model of loyalty.

Edmund is the illegitimate son of Gloucester, who successfully devises a scheme to besmirch Edgar and becomes his father's favorite. He serves the lust of both Goneril and Regan to further his ends. As he is dying in the last act, mortally wounded by a disguised Edgar, he admits his crimes in an inexplicable reversal of character, and tries to prevent the hanging of Cordelia that he has arranged. "The wheel has come full circle; I am here," he remarks in the moments before they carry him offstage.

Edgar is the legitimate son of the Earl of Gloucester, and the brother of illegitimate Edmund. He is rejected by his father when his father believes Edmund's scheme that Edgar has designs on Gloucester's life. Disguised as a beggar, Poor Tom, he helps his blind father. His final role, at the play's end, is to rule the kingdom.

Oswald is Goneril's servant, "a serviceable villain." He is hoping to murder Gloucester when instead he is murdered by Edgar.

The Fool is a jester entirely devoted to King Lear and Cordelia. He comments ironically on Lear's folly. He appears in Act I, scene four, and disappears in Act III, scene six. ❁

Critical Views on
King Lear

SAMUEL JOHNSON ON CORDELIA'S DEATH

[Dr. Samuel Johnson (1709–1784), one of the outstanding British literary figures of the eighteenth century, was a poet, essayist, critic, journalist, and lexicographer. His *Dictionary of the English Language* (1755) was the first major English dictionary to use historical quotations. In 1765 he wrote a monograph, *Preface to His Edition of Shakespeare,* and in the same year he edited a landmark annotated edition of Shakespeare's works. In this extract, Johnson comments on different issues that the play raises and strongly objects to Cordelia's death.]

The tragedy of Lear is deservedly celebrated among the dramas of Shakespeare. There is perhaps no play which keeps the attention so strongly fixed; which so much agitates our passions and interests our curiosity. The artful involutions of distinct interests, the striking opposition of contrary characters, the sudden changes of fortune, and the quick succession of events, fill the mind with a perpetual tumult of indignation, pity, and hope. There is no scene which does not contribute to the aggravation of the distress or conduct of the action, and scarce a line which does not conduce to the progress of the scene. So powerful is the current of the poet's imagination, that the mind, which once ventures within it, is hurried irresistibly along.

On the seeming improbability of Lear's conduct it may be observed, that he is represented according to histories at that time vulgarly received as true. And perhaps if we turn our thoughts upon the barbarity and ignorance of the age to which this story is referred, it will appear not so unlikely as while we estimate Lear's manners by our own. Such preference of one daughter to another, or resignation of dominion on such conditions, would be yet credible, if told of a pretty prince of Guinea or Madagascar. Shakespeare, indeed, by the mention of his earls and dukes, has given us the idea of times more civilised, and of life regulated by softer manners; and the truth is, that though he so nicely discriminates, and so minutely describes the characters of men, he commonly neglects and confounds the characters of ages, by mingling customs ancient and modern, English and foreign.

My learned friend Mr. Warton, who has in the *Adventurer* very minutely criticised this play, remarks, that the instances of cruelty are too savage and shocking, and that the intervention of Edmund destroys the simplicity of the story. These objections, may, I think, be answered, by repeating, that the cruelty of the daughters is an historical fact, to which the poet has added little, having only drawn it into a series by dialogue and action. But I am not able to apologise with equal plausibility for the extrusion of Gloucester's eyes, which seems an act too horrid to be endured in dramatick exhibition, and such as must always compel the mind to relieve its distress by incredulity. Yet let it be remembered that our authour well knew what would please the audience for which he wrote.

The injury done by Edmund to the simplicity of the action is abundantly recompensed by the addition of variety, by the art with which he is made to co-operate with the chief design, and the opportunity which he gives the poet of combining perfidy with perfidy, and connecting the wicked son with the wicked daughters, to impress this important moral, that villany is never at a stop, that crimes lead to crimes, and at last terminate in ruin.

But though this moral be incidentally enforced, Shakespeare has suffered the virtue of Cordelia to perish in a just cause, contrary to the natural ideas of justice, to the hope of the reader, and, what is yet more strange, to the faith of chronicles. Yet this conduct is justified by the Spectator, who blames Tate for giving Cordelia success and happiness in his alteration, and declares, that, in his opinion, "the tragedy has lost half its beauty." Dennis has remarked, whether justly or not, that, to secure the favourable reception of *Cato*, "the town was poisoned with much false and abominable criticism," and that endeavours had been used to discredit and decry poetical justice. A play in which the wicked prosper, and the virtuous miscarry, may doubtless be good, because it is a just representation of the common events of human life: but since all reasonable beings naturally love justice, I cannot easily be persuaded, that the observation of justice makes a play worse; or, that if other excellencies are equal, the audience will not always rise better pleased from the final triumph of persecuted virtue.

In the present case the publick has decided. Cordelia, from the time of Tate, has always retired with victory and felicity. And, if my sensations could add any thing to the general suffrage, I might relate, that I was many years ago so shocked by Cordelia's death, that I know not whether I ever endured to read again the last scenes of the play till I undertook to revise them as an editor.

There is another controversy among the criticks concerning this play. It is disputed whether the predominant image in Lear's disordered mind be the loss of his kingdom or the cruelty of his daughters. Mr. Murphy, a very judicious critick, has evinced by induction of particular passages, that the cruelty of his daughters is the primary source of his distress, and that the loss of royalty affects him only as a secondary and subordinate evil; he observed with great justness, that Lear would move our compassion but little, but did we not rather consider the injured father than the degraded king.

—Samuel Johnson, *The Plays of William Shakespeare,* vol. 6 (London: J. & R. Tonson, 1768): p. 158.

CHARLES LAMB ON *KING LEAR* AS A PLAY BEYOND THE STAGE

[The perceptive literary critic and writer Charles Lamb (1775–1834) is best-known for his "Essays of Elia," and *Tales of Shakespear,* a retelling of the plays for children, which he published with his sister Mary Lamb. In this extract Lamb argues that *King Lear* is the play beyond all art.]

⟨T⟩o see Lear acted,—to see an old man tottering about the stage with a walking-stick, turned out of doors by his daughters in a rainy night, has nothing in it but what is painful and disgusting. We want to take him into shelter and relieve him. That is all the feeling which the acting of Lear ever produced in me. But the Lear of Shakspeare cannot be acted. The contemptible machinery by which they mimic the storm which he goes out in, is not more inadequate to represent the horrors of the real elements, than any actor can be to represent Lear: they might more easily propose to personate the Satan of Milton upon a stage, or one of Michael Angelo's terrible figures. The greatness of Lear is not in corporal dimension, but in intellectual: the explosions of his passion are terrible as a volcano: they are storms turning up and disclosing to the bottom that sea, his mind, with all its vast riches. It is his mind which is laid bare. This case of flesh and blood seems too insignificant to be thought on; even as he himself neglects it. On the stage we see nothing but corporal infirmities and weakness, the impotence of rage; while we read it, we see not Lear, but we are Lear,—we are in his mind, we are sustained by a grandeur which baffles the malice of daughters and storms; in the aberrations of his reason, we discover a mighty irregular power of reasoning, immethodized from the ordinary purposes of life, but exerting its powers, as the wind blows where it listeth, at will upon the corruptions and abuses of mankind. What have looks, or tones, to do with that sublime identification of his age with that of the *heavens themselves,* when in his reproaches to them for conniving at the injustice of his children, he reminds them that "they themselves are old." What gesture shall we appropriate to this? What has the voice or the eye to do with such things? But the play is beyond all art, as the tamperings with it shew: it is too hard and stony; it must have love-scenes, and a happy ending. It is not enough that Cordelia is a daughter, she must shine as a lover, too. Tate has put his hook in the nostrils of this Leviathan, for Garrick and his followers, the showmen of the scene, to draw the mighty beast about more easily. A happy ending!—as if the living martyrdom that Lear had gone through,—the flaying of his feelings alive, did not make a fair dismissal from the stage of life the only decorous thing for him. If he is to live and be happy after, if he could sustain the world's burden after, why all this pudder and preparation,—why torment us with all this unnecessary sympathy? As if the childish pleasure of getting his gilt robes and sceptre again could tempt him to act over again his misused station,—as if at his years, and with his experience, anything was left but to die.

Lear is essentially impossible to be represented on a stage.

—Charles Lamb, "On the Tragedies of Shakspeare, Considered with Reference to Their Fitness for Stage Representation" [1812], *The Works of Charles and Mary Lamb*, vol. 1, edited by E. V. Lucas (London: Methuen, 1903): p. 107.

WILLIAM HAZLITT ON SHAKESPEARE AND THE LOGIC OF PASSION

[William Hazlitt (1778–1830) is an English writer best remembered for his essays. Among his many works are *Lectures on the English Poets* (1818), *Lectures on the English Comic Writers* (1819), and *Liber Amoris,* in which he describes the suffering of a love affair that ended disastrously. In this extract taken from *Characters of Shakespear's Plays* (1817), Hazlitt praises the play as Shakespeare's great masterpiece in the logic of passion.]

We wish that we could pass this play over, and say nothing about it. All that we can say must fall far short of the subject; or even of what we ourselves conceive of it. To attempt to give a description of the play itself or of its effect upon the mind, is mere impertinence: yet we must say something.—It is then the best of all Shakespear's plays, for it is the one in which he was most in earnest. He was here fairly caught in the web of his own imagination. The passion which he has taken as his subject is that which strikes its root deepest into the human heart; of which the bond is the hardest to be unloosed; and the cancelling and tearing to pieces of which gives the greatest revulsion to the frame. This depth of nature, this force of passion, this tug and war of the elements of our being, this firm faith in filial piety, and the giddy anarchy and whirling tumult of the thoughts at finding this prop failing it, the contrast between the fixed, immoveable basis of natural affection, and the rapid, irregular starts of imagination, suddenly wrenched from all its accustomed holds and resting-places in the soul, this is what Shakespear has given, and what nobody else but he could give. So we believe.—The mind of Lear, staggering between the weight of attachment and the hurried movements of passion, is like a tall ship driven about by the winds, buffetted by the furious waves, but that still rides above the storm, having its anchor fixed in the bottom of the sea; or it is like the sharp rock circled by the eddying whirlpool that foams and beats against it, or like the solid promontory pushed from its basis by the force of an earthquake.

The character of Lear itself is very finely conceived for the purpose. It is the only ground on which such a story could be built with the greatest truth and effect. It is his rash haste, his violent impetuosity, his blindness to everything but the dictates of his passions or affections, that produces all his misfortunes, that aggravates his impatience of them, that enforces our pity for him. The part which Cordelia bears in the scene is extremely beautiful: the story is almost told in the first words she utters. We see at once the precipice on which the poor old king stands from his own extravagant and credulous importunity, the indiscreet simplicity of her love (which, to be sure, has a little of her father's obstinacy in it) and the hollowness of her sister's pretensions. Almost the first burst of that noble tide of passion, which runs through the play, is in the remonstrance of Kent to his royal master on the injustice of his sentence against his youngest daughter—"Be Kent unmannerly, when Lear is mad!" This manly plainness, which draws down on him the displeasure of the unadvised king, is worthy of the fidelity with which he adheres to his fallen fortunes. The true character of the two eldest daughters, Regan and Gonerill (they are so thoroughly hateful that we do not even like to repeat their names) breaks out in their answer to Cordelia who desires them to treat their father well—"Prescribe not us our duties"—their hatred of advice being in proportion to their determination to do wrong, and to their hypocritical pretensions to do right. Their deliberate hypocrisy adds the last finishing to the odiousness of their characters. It is the absence of this detestable quality that is the only relief in the character of Edmund the Bastard, and that at times reconciles us to him. We are not tempted to exaggerate the guilt of his conduct, when he himself gives it up as a bad business, and writes himself down "plain villain." Nothing more can be said about it. His religious honesty in this respect is admirable. One speech of his is worth a million. His father, Gloster, whom he has just deluded with a forged story of his brother Edgar's designs against his life, accounts for his unnatural behaviour and the strange depravity of the times from the late eclipses in the sun and moon. Edmund, who is in the secret, says when he is gone—"This is the excellent foppery of the world, that when we are sick in fortune (often the surfeits of our own behaviour) we make guilty of our disasters the sun, the moon, and stars: as if we were villains on necessity; fools by heavenly compulsion; knaves, thieves, and treacherous by spherical predominance; drunkards, liars, and adulterers by an enforced obedience of planetary influence; and all that we are evil in, by a divine thrusting on. An admirable evasion of whore-master man, to lay his goatish disposition on the charge of a star! My father compounded with my mother under the Dragon's tail, and my nativity was under Ursa Major: so that it follows, I am rough and lecherous. Tut! I should have been what I am, had the maidenliest star in the firmament twinkled on my bastardising."—The whole character, its careless, light-hearted villainy, contrasted with the sullen, rancorous malignity of Regan and Gonerill, its connection with the conduct of the underplot, in which Gloster's persecution of one of his sons and the ingratitude of another, form a counterpart to the mistakes and misfortunes of Lear,—his double amour with the two sisters, and the share which he has in bringing about the fatal catastrophe, are all managed with an uncommon degree of skill and power.

It has been said, and we think justly, that the third act of *Othello* and the three first acts of *Lear,* are Shakespear's great master-pieces in the logic of passion: that they contain the highest examples not only of the force of individual passion, but of its dramatic vicissitudes and striking effects arising from the different circumstances and characters of the persons speaking. We see the ebb and flow of the feeling, its pauses and feverish starts, its impatience of opposition, its accumulating force when it has time to recollect itself, the manner in which it avails itself of every passing word or gesture, its haste to repel insinuation, the alternate contraction and dilatation of the soul, and all "the dazzling fence of controversy" in this mortal combat with poisoned weapons, aimed at the heart, where each wound is fatal.

—William Hazlitt, *Characters of Shakespear's Plays* (London: Macmillian 1817): pp. 94–97.

LEO TOLSTOY ON SHAKESPEARE'S FAILURE

[Leo Nikolayevich Tolstoy (1828–1910) is one of the world's greatest novelists; his works include the masterpieces *War and Peace* and *Anna Karenina.* A deeply contradictory man, Tolstoy abandoned his career as a writer of fiction to become a radical Christian. Toward the end of his life, Tolstoy wrote a polemic against Shakespeare, from which this extract is taken. Tolstoy expresses his belief that Shakespeare fails in portraying realistic characters.]

It is not enough to say that Shakespeare's characters are placed in tragic positions which are impossible, do not flow from the course of events, are inappropriate to time and space. These personages, besides this, act in a way that is out of keeping with their definite characters, and is quite arbitrary. It is generally asserted that in Shakespeare's dramas the characters are especially well expressed, that, notwithstanding their vividness, they are many-sided, like those of living people; that, whilst exhibiting the characteristics of a given individual, they at the same time wear the features of man in general; it is usual to say that the delineation of character in Shakespeare is the height of perfection.

This is asserted with much confidence, and repeated by all as indisputable truth; but, however much I endeavoured to find confirmation of this in

Shakespeare's dramas, I always found the opposite. In reading any of Shakespeare's dramas whatever I was, from the very first, instantly convinced that he was lacking in the most important, if not the only, means of portraying characters—individuality of language, i.e., the style of speech of every person being natural to his character. This is absent from Shakespeare. All his characters speak, not their own, but always one and the same Shakespearean pretentious and unnatural language, in which not only they could not speak, but in which no living man ever has spoken or does speak.

No living men could or can say as Lear says—that he would divorce his wife in the grave should Regan not receive him; or that the heavens would crack with shouting; or that the winds would burst; or that the wind wishes to blow the land into the sea; or that the curled waters wish to flood the shore, as the gentleman describes the storm; or that it is easier to bear one's grief; and the soul leaps over many sufferings when grief finds fellowship; or that Lear has become childless whilst I am fatherless, as Edgar says, or use similar unnatural expressions with which the speeches of all the characters in all Shakespeare's dramas overflow.

Again, it is not enough that all the characters speak in a way in which no living men ever did or could speak—they all suffer from a common intemperance of language. Those who are in love, who are preparing for death, who are fighting, who are dying, all alike speak much and unexpectedly about subjects utterly inappropriate to the occasion, being evidently guided rather by consonances and play of words than by thoughts. They speak all alike. Lear raves exactly as does Edgar when feigning madness. Both Kent and the fool speak alike. The words of one of the personages might be placed in the mouth of another, and by the character of the speech it would be impossible to distinguish who speaks. If there is a difference in the speech of Shakespeare's various characters, it lies merely in the different dialogues which are pronounced for these characters again by Shakespeare and not by themselves. Thus Shakespeare always speaks for Kings in one and the same inflated, empty language. Also in one and the same Shakespearean, artificially sentimental language speak all the women who are intended to be poetic—Juliet, Desdemona, Cordelia, Imogen, Marina. In the same way also it is Shakespeare alone who speaks for his villains—Richard, Edmund, Iago, Macbeth, expressing for them those vicious feelings which villains never express. Yet more similar are the speeches of the madmen with their horrible words and those of fools with their mirthless puns. So that in Shakespeare there is no language of living individuals—that language which in the drama is the chief means of setting forth characters. If gesticulation be also a means of expressing character, as in *ballets,* this is only a secondary means. Moreover, if the characters speak at random and in a random way, and all in one and the same diction, as is the case in Shakespeare's work, then even the action of gesticulation is wasted. Therefore, whatever the blind panegyrists of Shakespeare may say, in Shakespeare there is no expression of character. Those personages who in his dramas stand out as characters, are characters borrowed by him from former works which served as the foundation of his dramas, and they are mostly depicted, not only by the dramatic method, which consists in making each person speak with his own diction, but in the epic method of one person describing the features of another.

The perfection with which Shakespeare expresses character is asserted chiefly on the ground of the characters of Lear, Cordelia, Othello, Desdemona, Falstaff, Hamlet. But all these characters, as well as all the others, instead of belonging to Shakespeare, are taken by him from dramas, chronicles, and romances anterior to him. All these characters not only are not rendered more powerful by him, but in most cases they are weakened and spoilt. This is very striking in this drama of *King Lear,* which we are examining, taken by him from the drama *King Leir,* by an unknown author. The characters of this drama, that of King Leir, and especially of Cordelia, not only were not created by Shakespeare, but have been strikingly weakened and deprived of force by him, as compared with their appearance in the older drama.

—Leo Tolstoy, "On Shakespeare and the Drama" [Part II], translated by V. Tchertkoff and E. A., *Fortnightly Review* 87, no. 1 (January 1907): pp. 62–67.

A. C. BRADLEY ON LEAR'S INSANITY

[A. C. Bradley (1851–1935) was the leading British Shakespeare scholar of his time. He taught at the University of Liverpool, the University of Glasgow, and at Oxford University. This extract, which discusses Lear's insanity, is taken from his famous book, *Shakespearean Tragedy* (1904).]

Much has been written on the representation of insanity in *King Lear,* and I will confine myself to one or two points which may have escaped notice. The most obvious symptom of Lear's insanity, especially in its first stages, is of course the domination of a fixed idea. Whatever presents itself to his senses, is seized on by this idea and compelled to express it; as for example in those words, already quoted, which first show that his mind has actually given way:

> Hast thou given all
> To thy two daughters? And art thou come to this?

But it is remarkable that what we have here is only, in an exaggerated and perverted form, the very same action of imagination that, just before the breakdown of reason, produced those sublime appeals:

> O heavens,
> If you do love old men, if your sweet sway
> Allow obedience, if yourselves are old,
> Make it your cause;

and:

> Rumble thy bellyful! Spit, fire! spout rain!
> Nor rain, wind, thunder, fire, are my daughters:
> I tax not you, you elements, with unkindness;
> I never gave you kingdom, call'd you children,
> You owe me no subscription: then let fall
> Your horrible pleasure; here I stand, your slave,
> A poor, infirm, weak, and despised old man:
> But yet I call you servile ministers,
> That have with two pernicious daughters join'd
> Your high engender'd battles 'gainst a head
> So old and white as this. O! O! 'tis foul!

Shakespeare, long before this, in the *Midsummer Night's Dream,* had noticed the resemblance between the lunatic, the lover, and the poet; and the partial truth that genius is allied to insanity was quite familiar to him. But he presents here the supplementary half-truth that insanity is allied to genius.

He does not, however, put into the mouth of the insane Lear any such sublime passages as those just quoted. Lear's insanity, which destroys the coherence, also reduces the poetry of his imagination. What it stimulates is that power of moral perception and reflection which had already been quickened by his sufferings. This, however partial and however disconnectedly used, first appears, quite soon after the insanity has declared itself, in the idea that the naked beggar represents truth and reality, in contrast with those conventions, flatteries, and corruptions of the great world, by which Lear has so long been deceived and will never be deceived again:

> Is man no more than this? Consider him well. Thou owest the worm no silk,
> the beast no hide, the sheep no wool, the cat no perfume. Ha! here's three
> on's are sophisticated: thou art the thing itself.

Lear regards the beggar therefore with reverence and delight, as a person who is in the secret of things, and he longs to question him about their causes. It is this same strain of thought which much later (IV. vi.), gaining far greater force, though the insanity has otherwise advanced, issues in those famous Timon-like speeches which make us realise the original strength of the old King's mind. And when this strain, on his recovery, unites with the streams of repentance and love, it produces that serene renunciation of the world, with its power and glory and resentments and revenges, which is expressed in the speech (V. iii.):

> No, no, no, no! Come, let's away to prison:
> We two alone will sing like birds i' the cage:
> When thou dost ask me blessing, I'll kneel down,
> And ask of thee forgiveness: so we'll live,
> And pray, and sing, and tell old tales, and laugh
> At gilded butterflies, and hear poor rogues
> Talk of court news; and we'll talk with them too.
> Who loses, and who wins; who's in, who's out;
> And take upon's the mystery of things,
> As if we were God's spies: and we'll wear out,
> In a wall'd prison, packs and sects of great ones,
> That ebb and flow by the moon.

This is that renunciation which is at the same time a sacrifice offered to the gods, and on which the gods themselves throw incense; and, it may be, it would never have been offered but for the knowledge that came to Lear in his madness.

—A. C. Bradley, *Shakespearean Tragedy* (London: Macmillan, 1904): pp. 291–293.

STEPHEN BOOTH ON SHAKESPEARE'S AUDIENCE

[Stephen Booth, Professor of English at the University of California, Berkeley, is the author of *An Essay on Shakespeare's Sonnets*, *The Book Called Holinshed's Chronicles*, and *King Lear, Macbeth: Indefinition and Tragedy*, from which this extract is taken. He declares that Shakespeare's audience is like Lear.]

Shakespeare's audience is like Lear. Even before Shakespeare displays the embryo of a *Gorboduc-Cinderella* hybrid, we have already begun to act like Lear. The first words of the play focus our attention on Albany and Cornwall; as the play progresses, a series of beckoning hints of a coming clash between the two dukes (2.1.10–11, 25–27; 3.1.19–29) misleads us down a path to nowhere and does nothing to prepare us for the conflict between the two duchesses. More obviously symptomatic of our Lear-likeness are the character assessments we make during the conversation about Edmund's bastardizing (1.1.7–32). A moment later an audience will instantly assess Lear and join him in evaluating his three children on the basis of a few words; the audience will evaluate the children correctly; Lear will evaluate them incorrectly. The audience will evaluate the father correctly but inadequately. And the audience will be contemptuous of Lear's faith in conclusions reached on such meager, arbitrarily limited evidence. What we see Lear do during the test is what all audiences do always; what is more, before *this* audience first meets Lear, it has already made character assessments as faulty as Lear's. The division scene echoes the details of the opening conversation in which a casually autocratic parent ("He hath been out nine years, and away he shall again"—1.1.31–32) evaluates his children ("I have a son, sir, by order of law, some year elder than this who yet is no dearer in my account"—18–19). Gloucester's early speeches invite their audience to register him as a brutal oaf (an accurate but insufficient estimate) and Edmund as the humbly patient victim of his father's insensitivity (as erroneous an estimate as Lear's of Goneril and Regan).

Even our evaluations of the play are unfixed. Whenever we find fault with something Shakespeare does in *King Lear,* the alternative turns out to be in some way less acceptable. The plotting of *King Lear* invites adverse criticisms, but what Lear says to Kent on the heath might well be said to anyone who accepts even the more obvious of the invitations:

> Thou'dst shun a bear;
> But if thy flight lay toward the roaring sea,
> Thou'dst meet the bear i' th' mouth.
> (3.4.9–11)

Take, for example, the usually disturbing behavior of Edgar, who seems to be torturing his father by not revealing his identity: when Edgar at last does reveal his identity, the news kills Gloucester instantly. The crowning example, of course, is the end of the play—where we wish events otherwise than they are and where remedy would give more discomfort than the disease.

King Lear turns out to be faithless to the chronicle accounts of Lear, but its perfidy is sudden; the movement of the plot is toward a happy ending. I expect that every audience has felt the impulses that drove Nahum Tate to give *Lear* its promised end and led Samuel Johnson to applaud the deed. But Tate, who called Shakespeare's play "a Heap of Jewels, unstrung, and unpolished," made wholesale changes; after he had strung and polished the treasure he had seized, he had a new heap of jewels altogether. I doubt that many audiences could feel comfortable with a production that made sensible revision of the ending but left the play otherwise as Shakespeare wrote it. Rather than "rise better pleased from the final triumph of persecuted virtue," such an audience would probably value finality over triumph, and echo Kent:

Vex not his ghost. O, let him pass! He hates him
That would upon the rack of this tough world
Stretch him out longer.

(5.3.314–16)

To allow Lear and Cordelia to retire with victory and felicity would be to allow *more* to occur, would be to allow the range of our consideration and of
our standards of evaluation to dilate infinitely. It would be a strong man
whose natural ideas of justice and hopes for a happy resolution could out-
weigh his more basic need—his simple need of an ending—if, instead of Tate,
he had seen Shakespeare.

> —Stephen Booth, *King Lear, Macbeth: Indefinition and Tragedy* (New
> Haven: Yale University Press, 1983): pp. 68–70.

ROSALIE COLIE ON EDGAR'S BIBLICAL ECHOES

[Rosalie Colie taught at Barnard College, Oxford, Yale, and Toronto
University. At the time of her death in 1972, she was chairman of the
Department of Comparative Literature at Brown University. She is
the author of *Paradoxia Epidemica: The Resources of Kind, Shake-
speare's Living Art,* and *Atlantic Wall and Other Poems.* In this essay,
taken from her book *Some Facets of King Lear: Essays in Prismatic
Criticism,* she discusses the biblical echoes of Edgar's statement:
Ripeness is all.]

In the very ecstasy of madness, Lear found some reason, both to accept his
plight and his responsibility for that plight, and to accept the harsh justice of
men's lives. Edgar's speech to his father makes Lear's wisdom manageable in
aphorism, and carries some of the weight of the 39th Psalm, the one used in
the burial service: 'O spare me a little, that I may recover my strength, before
I go hence, and be no more seen.' Quite simply, Edgar states the stoical formulation to which Lear had come independently:

> Men must endure
> Their going hence, even as their coming hither:
> Ripeness is all.

(5.2.9–11)

All men must ultimately go to their long home, and cannot alter the date of
their going thither. Gloucester lives to die upon the revelation of reconcilia-
tion, while Lear, secured by his madness, lives to experience Edgar's terrifying
truth, that there is always something worse than what at any given moment

seems 'the worst.' He lives, then, to die upon the half-realized recognition that his selfless daughter has been gratuitously slain. Birth and death coincide: as Gloucester was careless in begetting Edmund, Edmund was careless in Cordelia's dispatching. 'Coming hither' is always involved in 'going hence.' As we see them in this play, goings hence are as ambiguous, as undignified, as unfair, as chancy as it is possible for them to be.

> For nether doeth man knowe his time, but as the fishes, which are taken in an evil net, and as the birdes that are caught in the snare: so are the children of men snared in the evil time when it falleth upon them suddenly.
>
> (Eccles. 9:12)

Those who try to die in their own time—Lear and Gloucester—are taken suddenly, at crucial moments between joy and grief; those who take others' lives—Cornwall, Regan, Goneril, Edmund—are caught in their own snares. The old die with the dignity of having borne most; such a death is, in the play's system of rewards, an honourable one. Their deaths become them, because they have learnt such hard endurance in their lives.

Throughout this play, the notion of a transcendent deity is not invoked. There is none of the overt reference, even by conventional accident, to God and His Son, such as is found in *Macbeth* or *Hamlet*. When 'the gods' are invoked, they are questioned and even jeered at; nor are stars admitted as a supernatural force. Again and again, the audience is brought to realize the extremity of 'the thing itself,' or, to realize that man is totally unaccommodated, can count on nothing, has no governance over his own fate. All he can do is be patient, endure, try to ripen: the most he can do for others is to realize that in their plight his own is involved. 'Ripeness' is self-realization, realization of responsibility for one's self and for others—the realization as well that such realization carries absolutely no guarantee of happiness. As Kent's life shows, or Cordelia's, the proper exercise of responsibility is just that—and no more than that. In this play, all that is certain is that irresponsibility breeds destruction. As Edgar says to Edmund, in the tones of Deuteronomy, Wisdom 11:13, and Wisdom 12:23, of their father's responsibility in his, and their, fate,

> The Gods are just, and of our pleasant vices
> Make instruments to plague us;
> The dark and vicious place where thee he got
> Cost him his eyes.
>
> (5.3.170–3)

But, we note, 'The dark and vicious place' was not the direct cause of disaster to Gloucester and his family alone; it could also be said to have cost Cordelia *her* life—and she was entirely unconnected with Gloucester's pleasant vices. Edgar speaks in the *sententiae* of justice with an echo, perhaps, of Matthew 5:28–29 and 6:23, and though we can say, with him, that Gloucester's fate is related to his vice, we cannot apply such generalization absolutely, either to

Gloucester or to the other characters woven with Gloucester into the web of the play's disasters. Ruin overtakes the good as inexorably as it does the wicked: Cordelia's tongue-tied truthfulness and Kent's sturdy honesty are by no stretch of the imagination just causes for their suffering. Indeed, Cordelia is most nearly the morality figure in the play, as she literally turns into the charity of which she speaks:

> No blown ambition doth our arms incite,
> But love, dear love . . .
>
> (4.4.27–8)

Her godliness was unmistakably proclaimed a line or so earlier:

> O dear father!
> It is thy business that I go about . . .
> (4.4.23–4)

But all this virtue, all this courage, generosity, innocence, and charity, cannot save Cordelia: she is involved, like all the rest, in the inexplicable vicissitudes of human life and lot, insisted on throughout the length of the play. For that is the point of *King Lear*, surely: that, as the Psalmist proclaims, man is inexorably and inextricably bound in with other men, brought to trial whether or not he deserves it. Man has no choice but to endure his life with such strengths as he can muster, and in his endurance lies his value as a man. Each man makes his choice between moral dignity and moral dishonour: those who choose dignity (Kent, the Fool, Cordelia, Cornwall's servant, Albany, Edgar) relinquish safety and advantage to become more admirable than those who seek their own without regard to others' needs. And that is all one can say. The rewards of the good are simply their comfortless virtues.

—Rosalie Colie, "The Energies of Endurance: Biblical Echo in *King Lear*." In *Some Facets of King Lear: Essays in Prismatic Criticism* (Toronto: Toronto University Press, 1974): pp. 134–136.

Plot Summary of
Macbeth

The three witches, or Weird Sisters, briefly set the tone of *Macbeth* in **Act I,** scene one. In the next scene, King Duncan of Scotland, with his sons Malcolm and Donalbain, receives a report from a sergeant of the royal army of a victory over an army of rebels. The sergeant also talks about the heroic deeds of "brave Macbeth," who slew the rebel Macdonwald. A Norwegian army has reinforced the rebel forces. Having heard of the disloyalty of the Thane of Cawdor ("Thane" is an honorific title like "Earl" or "Lord"), Duncan orders his execution and plans to reward Macbeth with that title.

In scene three, Macbeth and Banquo encounter the three witches, who greet Macbeth three times: first, as Thane of Glamis (his present title), then as Thane of Cawdor, and last as one that shall be "King hereafter." The witches also prophesy that although Banquo will never be a king, his descendants will. With these words they vanish, leaving Macbeth and Banquo wondering in awe about their words. The emissaries from Duncan arrive, and Macbeth learns that he has been made Thane of Cawdor (fulfilling the witches' first prophesy). This partial confirmation of the witches' words prompts Macbeth's murderous ambition, and he begins to think of regicide. He articulates his ambivalent feelings in a monologue that shows the magnitude of Macbeth's inner conflict.

In scene four, King Duncan receives news of the execution of the Thane of Cawdor. When Macbeth and Banquo enter, Duncan praises them. However, the King names his son Malcolm as his successor; Macbeth realizes that this would keep him from the throne. Duncan and his entire retinue intend to visit Macbeth at his castle at Inverness. Macbeth also departs but with his thoughts turned to murder.

Lady Macbeth, Macbeth's wife, is introduced in scene five, when she reads a letter from Macbeth in which he describes his encounter with the Weird Sisters and the fulfillment of their first prophecy. Since she feels that her husband may be too weak to kill Duncan, she vows to goad him on to murder. As soon as Macbeth arrives, she suggests that the King be killed that night and speaks of the murder as a foregone act. She politely greets Duncan and Banquo when they arrive in scene six. Amidst preparations for a banquet in honor of the King, the Macbeth couple prepares for the murder. Macbeth's internal crisis intensifies, whereas Lady Macbeth denounces all his hesitations. She suggests that the two chamberlains who guard the King be drugged with wine and then afterward blamed for the murder.

Night has fallen in **Act II.** Banquo and his son Fleance enter with a torch, and we learn that Banquo cannot sleep because of "cursed thoughts."

Macbeth enters, and in conversation with Banquo about the prophesy, he pretends indifference. He hints, though, that he could ask Banquo for a favor, and the latter makes clear that he will be glad to help if the favor does not involve any dishonorable enterprise. Banquo and Fleance leave the stage, and Macbeth imagines he sees a dagger in the air, pointing him to the King's chamber. He cannot tell if that sign is "a false creation,/Proceding from the heat-oppressed brain" or a prophetic sign. Macbeth goes to murder Duncan offstage.

In scene two, Lady Macbeth awaits her husband's return. Bewildered with horror after the murder is committed, Macbeth returns with the bloody daggers in his hand. He thinks he has heard a voice cry, "Sleep no more! Macbeth does murder sleep." Lady Macbeth has to take the weapon back so that the sleeping servants can be incriminated. A knocking at the castle gate brings events to a climax. Macbeth stands immobilized by his imagination and utters memorable words: "To know my deed, 'twere best not know myself."

The castle porter arouses from his sleep to answer the knocking at the gate in scene three. He delivers an amusing monologue in which he acts as if he is a porter in hell. Finally he opens the door to admit Macduff and Lenox, who are shortly afterward greeted by Macbeth. While Macduff goes to the room to wake up the King, Macbeth and Lenox engage in small talk about the terrible storm that took place the previous night. Macduff re-enters, screaming. Lenox and Macbeth go to the room, and Macbeth, pretending he is in a rage, slaughters the two drunk servants. Lady Macbeth faints; the King's two sons, Malcolm and Donalbain, when they find out about the murder of their father, agree to flee from Scotland.

The final scene of Act II takes place outside Macbeth's castle. Ross and an old man talk about the unnatural happenings of the previous night. Apparently, the King's horses turned wild, broke their stalls, and dashed out. The Old Man says: "Tis said they eat each other." Macduff enters and brings news for Ross (and for the audience) that Malcolm and Donalbain have fled; this puts suspicion for the murder upon them. The sovereignty, as the witches promised, will fall upon Macbeth.

In **Act III,** scene one, Banquo suspects that Macbeth may have murdered Duncan. Macbeth and Lady Macbeth enter and ask for Banquo's presence at a banquet in honor of Macbeth. Banquo promises he will attend after he comes back from a ride. Macbeth, offended by the witches' prophecy that Banquo's descendants will be kings, hires two assassins to kill Banquo and his son Fleance before they return that night.

In scene two, Lady Macbeth finds her position as Queen far less fortunate than she expected. In scene three, Banquo is killed by the murderers, but his son escapes. When Macbeth learns this at the banquet in the next scene, he is considerably shaken. The appearance of Banquo's ghost, visible only to Macbeth (like the dagger in Act II, scene one), so upsets Macbeth that Lady Macbeth has to dismiss the guests. Upon learning that Macduff is virtually in revolt, Macbeth decides to seek out the Weird Sisters a second time.

Two brief scenes conclude Act III. In scene five, we see the witches preparing for Macbeth's visit, and we learn how the English King Edward has welcomed Malcolm. In scene six, we see that Macduff is also there, hoping to raise an army to oppose Macbeth.

In **Act IV,** scene one, the witches show Macbeth three visions arising from a cauldron: an Armed Head warns him to be beware of Macduff; a Bloody Child promises him that "none of woman born/Shall harm Macbeth"; and a Crowned Child with a tree in his hand promises Macbeth that he shall not be vanquished until a forest, Birnam Wood, comes against him in his castle. He is pleased with the prophecies until the vision of a line of kings stretching "to th' crack of doom" appears. These future kings are of Banquo's lineage, not his; this confirms all of his worst fears. The witches vanish, and Lenox enters and informs Macbeth that Macduff has fled to England. Macbeth decides instantly that he has to kill Macduff's family.

Scene two shows Ross comforting Lady Macduff after her husband has fled. After Ross leaves, Macbeth's hired murderers arrive and kill her and her children. In the meantime (scene three), Macduff joins Malcolm in England and urges him to unseat Macbeth. Malcolm distrusts Macduff and puts him to the test. Finally persuaded of Macduff's loyalty, Malcolm reveals to him that the Earl of Northumberland's army of ten thousand is ready to attack Macbeth. Ross enters and reports the slaughter of Macduff's family, at which Macduff resolves to avenge them to "cure this deadly grief."

In the final act, **Act V,** the roles of Macbeth and Lady Macbeth reverse. As a doctor and a gentlewoman carefully watch Lady Macbeth and talk about her nocturnal walkings, she rubs her hands in a vain effort to wash the invisible blood off them. Though her behavior cannot be rationalized, the onlookers comprehend that something weighty lies on her conscious.

The next five scenes show proceedings for war. Scottish rebels approach Birnam Wood, where they are to meet English forces. Macbeth has fortified his castle, ready to defend it, although he lacks the loyalty of his own men.

Birnam Wood moves in scene four when Malcolm orders his solders to each cut down a tree branch and carry it as they march, thus "shadowing" the army's numbers from observers in Macbeth's castle. Lady Macbeth dies unlamented by Macbeth. His comment in a memorable speech is that "life's but a walking shadow. . . . a tale told by an idiot, full of sound and fury, signifying nothing."

In scene six, Malcolm reaches the castle. In the seventh scene, Macbeth goes into the open field to fight. He kills young Siward, son of the Earl of Northumberland; this convinces him of the invincibility promised by the witches. The final scene begins as Macbeth and Macduff face each other. When Macbeth boasts that no man born of a woman can hurt him, Macduff replies that he was "untimely ripp'd" from his mother's womb—born by cesarean section. This shakes Macbeth's confidence. In the duel, which moves off stage, Macduff kills Macbeth. When he returns, bearing the head of Macbeth, Malcolm is proclaimed the King of Scotland.

Why are we so irresistably drawn to Macbeth? Why does Macbeth raise our admiration? These are the questions critics have tried to answer down through the centuries. Perhaps the answer lies in the glimpses Macbeth gives us into his creator, William Shakespeare. The desolation of the play is conveyed to the readers through its hero's fantastic imagination, a mirror image of Shakespeare himself. ❀

List of Characters in
Macbeth

When we first meet him, **Macbeth** is Duncan's victorious general. But no sooner has he heard the witches' prophesy than he murders the king and commits a number of brutal killings. His feelings of inner solitude grow steadily with each of them. The "terrible dreams" pursue him, and "torture of the mind" gives him no peace. As he puts it: "Strange things I have in head, that will to hand,/which must be acted, ere thay may be scann'd."

Lady Macbeth is Macbeth's wife. At the beginning she is the one who leads while Macbeth follows. She urges him to commit the murders, questioning his manhood. Later, she collapses before Macbeth does and commits suicide.

Duncan is the "gracious" Scottish king whom Macbeth murders. He is presented as generous and loving.

Malcolm is the older son of Duncan. After his father is murdered, he flees from Macbeth's castle to England. Macduff joins him later, and they assemble the army to attack Macbeth. When the battle is over, Macduff gives Macbeth's head to Malcolm and proclaims him king.

Macduff is Thane of Fife. When he finds Duncan murdered in Macbeth's castle, he becomes suspicious and refuses to attend Macbeth's coronation celebration. In a cryptic way, the witches warn Macbeth of Macduff; according to their prophesy "none of a woman born shall harm Macbeth" (Macduff was delivered by cesarean section). Macduff is in England when the news of his wife and children's murder reaches him. In the final battle, he kills Macbeth.

Banquo is a Scottish gentleman who encounters the witches with Macbeth. In order to nullify the witches' prophesy that Banquo's descendants will be kings, Macbeth kills him. It is his ghost who appears at Macbeth's celebration; this disturbs Macbeth so profoundly that the other thanes notice.

Fleance is Banquo's son and heir, who escapes Macbeth's assassins. The witches insinuate that through Fleance, Banquo's descendants will eventually become kings.

The Witches, or Weird Sisters, are bearded women who are agents of Fate under the rule of the Goddess Hecate. Macbeth sees them twice. ❀

Critical Views on
Macbeth

SAMUEL JOHNSON ON *MACBETH*'S REALISM

[Dr. Samuel Johnson (1709–1784), one of the outstanding British literary figures of the eighteenth century, was a poet, essayist, critic, journalist, and lexicographer. His *Dictionary of the English Language* (1755) was the first major English dictionary to use historical quotations. In 1765 he wrote a monograph, *Preface to His Edition of Shakespeare,* and in the same year he edited a landmark annotated edition of Shakespeare's works. In this extract, Johnson comments on different issues that the play raises.]

This play is deservedly celebrated for the propriety of its fictions, and solemnity, grandeur, and variety of its action; but it has no nice discriminations of character, the events are too great to admit the influence of particular dispositions, and the course of the action necessarily determines the conduct of the agents.

The danger of ambition is well described; and I know not whether it may not be said in defence of some parts which now seem improbable, that, in Shakespeare's time, it was necessary to warn credulity against vain and illusive predictions.

The passions are directed to their true end. Lady Macbeth is merely detested; and though the courage of Macbeth preserves some esteem, yet every reader rejoices at his fall.

—Samuel Johnson, *The Plays of William Shakespeare,* vol. 6 (London: J. & R. Tonson, 1768): p. 484.

SAMUEL TAYLOR COLERIDGE ON THE LACK OF PUNNING IN *MACBETH*

[In addition to being one of the greatest British poets of the early nineteenth century, Samuel Taylor Coleridge (1772–1834) was also a penetrating critic. His most famous critical work is *Biographia Literaria* (1817). In 1819 he delivered a series of lectures on Shakespeare, which were published posthumously in his *Literary Remains* (1836–39). In this extract he compares *Macbeth* with *Hamlet,* finding the former lacking in the punning.]

Macbeth stands in contrast throughout with *Hamlet;* in the manner of opening more especially. In the latter, there is a gradual ascent from the simplest forms of conversation to the language of impassioned intellect,—yet the intellect still remaining the seat of passion: in the former, the invocation is at once made to the imagination and the emotions connected therewith. Hence the movement throughout is the most rapid of all Shakespeare's plays; and hence also, with the exception of the disgusting passage of the Porter (Act ii, sc. 3.), which I dare pledge myself to demonstrate to be an interpolation of the actors, there is not, to the best of my remembrance, a single pun or play on words in the whole drama. I have previously given an answer to the thousand times repeated charge against Shakespeare upon the subject of his punning, and I here merely mention the fact of the absence of any puns in *Macbeth*, as justifying a candid doubt at least, whether even in these figures of speech and fanciful modifications of language, Shakespeare may not have followed rules and principles that merit and would stand the test of philosophic examination. And hence, also, there is an entire absence of comedy, nay, even of irony and philosophic contemplation in *Macbeth*,—the play being wholly and purely tragic. For the same cause, there are no reasonings of equivocal morality, which would have required a more leisurely state and a consequently greater activity of mind;—no sophistry of self-delusion,—except only that previously to the dreadful act, Macbeth mistranslates the recoilings and ominous whispers of conscience into prudential and selfish reasonings, and, after the deed done, the terrors of remorse into fear from external dangers,—like delirious men who run away from the phantoms of their own brains, or, raised by terror to rage, stab the real object that is within their reach:—whilst Lady Macbeth merely endeavours to reconcile his and her own sinkings of heart by anticipations of the worst, and an affected bravado in confronting them. In all the rest, Macbeth's language is the grave utterance of the very heart, conscience-sick, even to the last faintings of moral death. It is the same in all the other characters. The variety arises from rage, caused ever and anon by disruption of anxious thought, and the quick transition of fear into it.

> —Samuel Taylor Coleridge, "Notes on Macbeth" [1819], *Literary Remains*, vol. 2, edited by Henry Nelson Coleridge (London: Pickering, 1836): pp. 235–236.

GEORG BRANDES ON *MACBETH* IN COMPARISON TO *HAMLET*

[Georg Brandes (1842–1927) was a Danish critic and scholar who exerted a tremendous influence on the Scandinavian literary world. He wrote many scholarly studies, including monographs on Kierkegaard and Danish playwright Ludvig Holberg, and biographies of Shakespeare, Goethe, Voltaire, Julius Caesar, and Michelangelo. In this extract, taken from his study on Shakespeare, he compares *Hamlet* and *Macbeth*.]

There is much to indicate that an unbroken train of thought led Shakespeare from *Hamlet* to *Macbeth*. The personality of Macbeth is a sort of counterpart to that of Hamlet. The Danish prince's nature is passionate, but refined and thoughtful. Before the deed of vengeance which is imposed upon him he is restless, self-reproachful, and self-tormenting; but he never betrays the slightest remorse for a murder once committed, though he kills four persons before he stabs the King. The Scottish thane is the rough, blunt soldier, the man of action. He takes little time for deliberation before he strikes; but immediately after the murder he is attacked by hallucinations both of sight and hearing, and is hounded on, wild and vacillating and frenzied, from crime to crime. He stifles his self-reproaches and falls at last, after defending himself with the hopeless fury of the "bear tied to the stake."

Hamlet says:—

> And thus the native hue of resolution
> Is sicklied o'er with the pale cast of thought.

Macbeth, on the contrary, declares (iv. I)—

> From this moment
> The very firstlings of my heart shall be
> The firstlings of my hand.

They stand at opposite poles—Hamlet, the dreamer; Macbeth, the captain, "Bellona's bridegroom." Hamlet has a superabundance of culture and of intellectual power. His strength is of the kind that wears a mask; he is a master in the art of dissimulation. Macbeth is unsophisticated to the point of clumsiness; betraying himself when he tries to deceive. His wife has to beg him not to show a troubled countenance, but to "sleek o'er his rugged looks."

Hamlet is the born aristocrat: very proud, keenly alive to his worth, very self-critical—too self-critical to be ambitious in the common acceptation of the word. To Macbeth, on the contrary, a sounding title is honour, and a wreath on the head, a crown on the brow, greatness. When the Witches on the heath, and another witch, his wife in the castle, have held up before his eyes the glory of the crown and the power of the sceptre, he has found his great goal—a tangible prize in this life, for which he is willing to risk his welfare in "the life to come." Whilst Hamlet, with his hereditary right, hardly gives a thought to the throne of which he has been robbed, Macbeth murders his king, his benefactor, his guest, that he may plunder him and his sons of a chair with a purple canopy.

And yet there is a certain resemblance between Macbeth and Hamlet. One feels that the two tragedies must have been written close upon each other. In his first monologue (i. 7) Macbeth stands hesitating with Hamlet-like misgivings:—

> If it were done, when 't is done, then 't were well
> It were done quickly: if the assassination
> Could trammel up the consequence, and catch
> With his surcease success; that but this blow
> Might be the be-all and the end-all here,
> But here, upon this bank and shoal of time,—
> We'd jump the life to come.—But in these cases
> We still have judgment here

Hamlet says: Were we sure that there is no future life, we should seek death. Macbeth thinks: Did we not know that judgment would come upon us here, we should care little about the life to come. There is a kinship in these contradictory reflections. But Macbeth is not hindered by his cogitations. He pricks the sides of his intent, as he says, with the spur of ambition, well knowing that it will o'er-leap itself and fall. He cannot resist when he is goaded onward by a being superior to himself, a woman.

Like Hamlet, he has imagination, but of a more timorous and visionary cast. It is through no peculiar faculty in Hamlet that he sees his father's ghost; others had seen it before him and see it with him. Macbeth constantly sees apparitions that no one else sees, and hears voices that are inaudible to others.

When he has resolved on the king's death he sees a dagger in the air:—

> Is this a dagger which I see before me,
> The handle toward my hand? Come, let me clutch thee:—
> I have thee not, and yet I see thee still.
> Are thou not, fatal vision, sensible
> To feeling, as to sight? or art thou but
> A dagger of the mind, a false creation,
> Proceeding from the heat-oppressed brain?

Directly after the murder he has an illusion of hearing:—

> Methought I heard a voice cry, "Sleep no more!
> Macbeth does murder sleep."

And, very significantly, Macbeth hears this same voice give him the different titles which are his pride:—

> Still it cried, "Sleep no more!" to all the house:
> "Glamis hath murder'd sleep, and therefore Cawdor
> Shall sleep no more, Macbeth shall sleep no more!"

Yet another parallel shows the kinship between the Danish and the Scottish tragedy. It is in these dramas alone that the dead leave their graves and reappear on the scene of life; in them alone a breath from the spirit-world reaches the atmosphere of the living. There is no trace of the supernatural either in *Othello* or in *King Lear.*

—Georg Brandes, *William Shakespeare: A Critical Study,* vol. 2, translated by William Archer and Mary Morison (London: William Heinemann, 1898): pp. 94–96.

A. C. Bradley on Macbeth's Imagination

[A. C. Bradley (1851–1935) was the leading British Shakespeare scholar of his time. He taught at the University of Liverpool, the University of Glasgow, and at Oxford University. This extract is taken from his famous book *Shakespearean Tragedy* (1904), which established him as the preeminent Shakespeare scholar of the early twentieth century and remains a classic of modern Shakespeare criticism. In it, Bradley makes an interesting observation that Macbeth's imagination is the best part of him.]

From this murky background stand out the two great terrible figures, who dwarf all the remaining characters of the drama. Both are sublime, and both inspire, far more than the other tragic heroes, the feeling of awe. They are never detached in imagination from the atmosphere which surrounds them and adds to their grandeur and terror. It is, as it were, continued into their souls. For within them is all that we felt without—the darkness of night, lit with the flame of tempest and the hues of blood, and haunted by wild and direful shapes, 'murdering ministers', spirits of remorse, and maddening visions of peace lost and judgment to come. The way to be untrue to Shakespeare here, as always, is to relax the tension of imagination, to conventionalize, to conceive Macbeth, for example, as a half-hearted cowardly criminal, and Lady Macbeth as a whole-hearted fiend.

These two characters are fired by one and the same passion of ambition; and to a considerable extent they are alike. The disposition of each is high, proud, and commanding. They are born to rule, if not to reign. They are peremptory or contemptuous to their inferiors. They are not children of light, like Brutus and Hamlet; they are of the world. We observe in them no love of country, and no interest in the welfare of anyone outside their family. Their habitual thoughts and aims are, and, we imagine, long have been, all of station and power. And though in both there is something, and in one much, of what is higher—honour, conscience, humanity—they do not live consciously in the light of these things or speak their language. Not that they are egoists, like Iago;

or, if they are egoists, theirs is an *egoïsme à deux*. They have no separate ambitions. They support and love one another. They suffer together. And if, as time goes on, they drift a little apart, they are not vulgar souls, to be alienated and recriminate when they experience the fruitlessness of their ambition. They remain to the end tragic, even grand.

So far there is much likeness between them. Otherwise they are contrasted, and the action is built upon this contrast. Their attitudes towards the projected murder of Duncan are quite different; and it produces in them equally different effects. In consequence, they appear in the earlier part of the play as of equal importance, if indeed Lady Macbeth does not overshadow her husband; but afterwards she retires more and more into the background, and he becomes unmistakably the leading figure. ⟨ . . . ⟩

Macbeth's better nature—to put the matter for clearness' sake too broadly—instead of speaking to him in the overt language of moral ideas, commands and prohibitions, incorporates itself in images which alarm and horrify. His imagination is thus the best of him, something usually deeper and higher than his conscious thoughts; and if he had obeyed it he would have been safe. But his wife quite misunderstands it, and he himself understands it only in part. The terrifying images which deter him from crime and follow its commission, and which are really the protest of his deepest self, seem to his wife the creations of mere nervous fear, and are sometimes referred by himself to the dread of vengeance or the restlessness of insecurity. His conscious or reflective mind, that is, moves chiefly among considerations of outward success and failure, while his inner being is convulsed by conscience. And his inability to understand himself is repeated and exaggerated in the interpretations of actors and critics, who represent him as a coward, cold-blooded, calculating, and pitiless, who shrinks from crime simply because it is dangerous, and suffers afterwards simply because he is not safe. In reality his courage is frightful. He strides from crime to crime, though his soul never ceases to bar his advance with shapes of terror, or to clamour in his ears that he is murdering his peace and casting away his 'eternal jewel.'

It is of the first importance to realize the strength, and also (what has not been so clearly recognized) the limits, of Macbeth's imagination. It is not the universal meditative imagination of Hamlet. He came to see in man, as Hamlet sometimes did, the 'quintessence of dust'; but he must always have been incapable of Hamlet's reflections on man's noble reason and infinite faculty, or of seeing with Hamlet's eyes 'this brave o'erhanging firmament, this majestical roof fretted with golden fire'. Nor could he feel, like Othello, the romance of war or the infinity of love. He shows no sign of any unusual sensitiveness to the glory or beauty in the world or the soul; and it is partly for this reason that we have no inclination to love him, and that we regard him with more of awe than of pity. His imagination is excitable and intense, but narrow. That which stimulates it is, almost solely, that which thrills with sudden, startling, and often supernatural fear.

—A. C. Bradley. *Shakespearean Tragedy* (London: Macmillan, 1904): pp. 321–325.

Wayne C. Booth on Macbeth's Destruction

[Wayne C. Booth is George W. Pullman professor of English at the University of Chicago. His first book, *The Rhetoric of Fiction* (1961), is a classic of modern criticism. His books include *Modern Dogma and the Rhetoric of Assent* (1974), *A Rhetoric of Irony* (1975), and *Critical Understanding: The Powers and Limits of Pluralism* (1979). In this article, Booth analyzes the destruction of Macbeth.]

Put even in its simplest terms, the problem Shakespeare gave himself in *Macbeth* was a tremendous one. Take a good man, a noble man, a man admired by all who know him—and destroy him, not only physically and emotionally, as the Greeks destroyed their heroes, but also morally and intellectually. As if this were not difficult enough as a dramatic hurdle, while transforming him into one of the most despicable mortals conceivable, maintain him as a tragic hero—that is, keep him so sympathetic that, when he comes to his death, the audience will pity rather than detest him and will be relieved to see him out of his misery rather than pleased to see him destroyed. Put in Shakespeare's own terms: take a "noble" man, full of "conscience" and "the milk of human kindness," and make of him a "dead butcher," yet keep him an object of pity rather than hatred. If we thus artificially reconstruct the problem as it might have existed before the play was written, we see that, in choosing these "terminal points" and these terminal intentions, Shakespeare makes almost impossible demands on his dramatic skill, although at the same time he insures that, if he succeeds at all, he will succeed magnificently. If the trick can be turned, it will inevitably be a great one.

One need only consider the many relative failures in attempts at similar "plots" and effects to realize the difficulties involved. When dramatists or novelists attempt the sympathetic-degenerative plot, almost always one or another of the following failures or transformations occurs: (1) The feeling of abhorrence for the protagonist becomes so strong that all sympathy is lost, and the play or novel becomes "punitive"—that is, the reader's or spectator's chief pleasure depends on his satisfaction in revenge or punishment. (2) The protagonist is never really made very wicked, after all; he only *seems* wicked by conventional (and, by implication, unsound) standards and is really a highly admirable reform-candidate. (3) The protagonist reforms in the end and avoids his proper punishment. (4) The book or play itself becomes a "wicked" work; that is, either deliberately or unconsciously the artist makes us side with his degenerated hero against "morality." If it is deliberate, we have propaganda works of one kind or another, often resembling the second type above; if it is unconscious, we get works whose immorality (as in pornographic or sadistic treatments of the good-girl-turned-whore, thief, or murderess) makes them unenjoyable as literature unless the reader or spectator temporarily or permanently relaxes his own standards of moral judgment. Any of these failures or transformations can be found in conjunction with the most frequent failure of all: the degeneration remains finally unexplained, unmotivated; the forces employed to destroy the noble man are found pitifully inadequate to make his fall seem credible. ⟨ . . . ⟩

The evil of his acts is thus built upon the knowledge that he is not a naturally evil man but a man who has every potentiality for goodness. This potentiality and its frustration are the chief ingredients of the tragedy of Macbeth. Macbeth is a man whose progressive external misfortunes seem to produce, and at the same time seem to be produced by, his parallel progression from great goodness to great wickedness. Our emotional involvement (which perhaps should not be simplified under the term "pity" or "pity and fear") is thus a combination of two kinds of regret: (1) We regret that any potentially good man should come to such a bad end: "What a pity that things should have gone this way, that things should *be* this way!" (2) We regret even more the destruction of this particular man, a man who is not only morally sympathetic but also intellectually and emotionally interesting. In eliciting both these kinds of regret to such a high degree, Shakespeare goes beyond his predecessors and establishes trends which are still working themselves out in literature. The first kind—never used at all by classical dramatists, who never employed a genuinely degenerative plot—has been attempted again and again by modern novelists. Their difficulty has usually been that they have relied too completely on a general humane response in the reader and too little on a realized prior height or potentiality from which to fall. The protagonists are shown succumbing to their environment—or, as in so many "sociological" novels, already succumbed—and the reader is left to himself to infer that something worth bothering about has gone to waste, that things might have been otherwise, that there is any real reason to react emotionally to the final destruction. The second kind—almost unknown to classical dramatists, whose characters are never "original" or "fresh" in the modern sense—has been attempted in ever greater extremes since Shakespeare, until one finds many works in which mere *interest* in particular characteristics completely supplants emotional response to *events* involving men with interesting characteristics. The pathos of Bloom for example, is an attenuated pathos, just as the comedy of Bloom is an attenuated comedy; one is not primarily moved to laughter or tears by events involving great characters, as in *Macbeth,* but rather one is primarily interested in details about characters. It can be argued whether this is a gain or a loss to literature, when considered in general. Certainly, one would rather read a modern novel like *Ulysses,* with all its faults on its head, than many of the older dramas or epics involving "great" characters in "great" events. But it can hardly be denied that one of Shakespeare's triumphs is his success in doing many things at once which lesser writers have since done only one at a time. He has all the generalized effect of a classical tragedy. We lament the "bad fortune" of a great man who has known good fortune. To this he adds the much more poignant (at least to us) pity one feels in observing the moral destruction of a great man who has once known goodness. And yet with all this he combines the pity one feels when one observes a highly characterized individual—whom one knows intimately, as it were, in whom one is *interested*—going to destruction. One difference between watching Macbeth go to destruction and watching the typical modern hero, whether in the drama (say, Willy Loman) or in the novel (say, Jake or any other of Hemingway's heroes), is that in *Macbeth* there is some "going." Willy Loman doesn't have very far to fall; he begins the play on the verge of suicide, and at the end of the play he has committed suicide. Even if we assume that the "beginning" is the time covered in the earliest of the flashbacks, we have not "far to go" from there to Willy's destruction. It is true that our contemporary willingness to exalt the potentialities of the average man makes Willy's fall seem to *us* a greater one than it really is, dramatically. But the reliance on convention will, of course, sooner or later dictate a decline in the play's effectiveness. *Macbeth* continues to be effective at least in part because everything necessary for a complete response to a complete action is given to us. A highly individualized, noble man is sent to complete moral, intellectual, and physical destruction.

—Wayne C. Booth, "Macbeth as Tragic Hero," *Journal of General Education* 6, no.1 (October 1951): pp. 17–25.

GRAHAM BRADSHAW ON *MACBETH*'S TWO MARRIAGES

[Graham Bradshaw is professor in English at University of St. Andrews. In this extract, taken from his book *Shakespeare's Scepticism* (1987), Bradshaw juxtaposes the two marriages in the play: Macbeth's and Macduff's.]

In certain respects the Macbeths' marriage is normative, and deeply touching in its essential domesticity. For Macbeth, even an appalling cry of agony can be accompanied by an unthinking acknowledgment of that corner of his mind which is not infected:

> O, full of Scorpions is my Minde, deare Wife . . .

'My dearest Love', 'dearest Chuck': the very casualness of such tenderness suggests how much these lovers can afford to take for granted in each other, and testifies to continual reciprocities of feeling—as does the tenderness of Lady Macbeth's breathtakingly simple language in the sleepwalking scene:

> Wash your hands, put on your Night-Gowne, looke not
> so pale . . .
> Come, come, come, come, give me your hand: What's done,
> cannot be undone. To bed, to bed, to bed.
>
> (5.1.60 f.)

Such intimacy is magnificently domestic, far removed from the heavens and hells of Grand Passion. In Lady Macbeth's case it is also clear that her collapse is in part the result of the increasing estrangement we saw her feeling in 3.2 ('why doe you keep alone?'); we might be reminded of Portia in *Julius Caesar,* who could not endure the breakdown of a trust and intimacy she had learned to take for granted.

But the intense bond contains its own solvent, in that preoccupation with manliness which the sleepwalking scene also recalls ('Fye, my Lord, fie, a Souldier, and affear'd?') and which proved so decisive in 1.7. The capacity for affection which Macbeth shows in his relations with his wife is also present in the generosity of his tributes to the gracious Duncan and the royal Banquo; but this potential lifeline to a larger community is severed within the marriage itself, which is at best a refuge or sanctuary, when it is not a campaign headquarters. The Macbeths' marriage neither establishes nor looks for any further connection with a community. Having no metaphysical dimension, representing no morally constructive aspiration, it is never more than—if sometimes not less than—'mating' at its most human and engaging. Macbeth lives vigorously in that 'Chaos' which Othello feared, and refuses to give credence to that need for value and significance which directed Othello's whole life. For all its attractive, normative aspects, this marriage remains socially, morally and of course literally sterile, providing no vantage from which Macbeth might assess his relations with others or with those parts of his own nature which Duncan would 'plant' and cultivate and which his wife fears. The marriage is in this sense *merely* natural.

As is well known, Shakespeare adjusted his sources to compress the length of Macbeth's reign and to highlight the practical and symbolic issue of childlessness. This was essential to the subtle and elaborate contrast with the

Macduffs—I should say contrasts, since Shakespeare contrasts the two men, the two women, and the couples' respective relations with each other and the larger world. For Macbeth, a 'deare Wife' takes precedence over all other allegiances, including those which dictate Macduff's behaviour. Lady Macduff—who is identified in the Folio as 'Macduffes Wife' and then becomes 'Wife'—provides another charged contrast: not only does she complain of her husband's unnaturalness, she is herself altogether *too* natural—so that our distress on her behalf might be expressed through the words she addresses to her poor, doomed son: 'Poore pratler, how thou talk'st' (4.2.63). Two men risk their lives in trying to persuade her to take her children away: 'I pray you schoole your selfe', pleads the desperate Rosse—but she will do nothing but talk, making her son the bewildered receptacle of her paralysing terror, self-pity and resentment:

> . . . He loves us not,
> He wants the naturall touch . . .
> (8–9)
> . . . Sirra, your Father's dead,
> And what will you do now? How will you live?
> (30–1)

This, in its helpless naturalness, is beyond her control or our censure; but we still notice how—like many another much wronged, abandoned single parent—she gives no thought to the likely effect such remarks will have on the boy.

And there is a wrenching psychological truthfulness in the way the poor lad picks up one word which has nagged at his mind since he heard his mother say, 'Our feares do make us Traitors'. 〈 . . . 〉

In the next scene this irony is given a particularly ferocious twist, when the incredulous Macduff discovers that his readiness to set King and Country before wife and family is what actually arouses Malcolm's suspicion:

> *Macduff:*   I have lost my Hopes.
> *Malcolm:*   Perchance even there where I did finde my doubts.
> Why in that rawnesse left you Wife, and Childe?
> Those precious Motives, those strong knots of Love,
> Without leave-taking . . .
> (4.3.24–8)

That echo may remind us that in his own hour of crisis Malcolm thought it best to 'shift away' without being 'daintie of leave-taking' (2.3.143–4). Here Malcolm displays another kind of prudence as he stalks, quizzes and tests Macduff: in seeing the need to be wary of Macbeth's 'trains', and in putting to work his knowledge that there *is* an 'Art, to finde the Mindes construction', Malcolm is less gracious than his father, and more astute. Where his father had committed himself to constructive acts of love and trust, the wary, frightened son loves and trusts nobody. As he tests Macduff we appraise both men, and the testing is far more elaborate than that in Holinshed. But to see this we need to recognise why Shakespeare has placed this 'English' scene between the scene in Fife and the scene in which Lady Macbeth is observed.

—Graham Bradshaw, *Shakespeare's Scepticism* (New York: St. Martin's Press, 1987): pp. 236–240.

HAROLD BLOOM ON *MACBETH*'S GNOSTICISM

[Harold Bloom, the editor of this series, is Sterling Professor of the Humanities at Yale University and Berg Professor of English at New York University. He is the author of more than 20 books and the editor of over 40 anthologies of both literature and literary criticism. His latest book, *Shakespeare: the Invention of the Human*, was published in November 1998. In this extract, taken from the introduction to a critical anthology on *Macbeth* in the Chelsea House series MODERN CRITICAL INTERPRETATIONS, Bloom explores Macbeth's gnostic declarations.]

Critics remark endlessly about two aspects of *Macbeth*, its obsession with "time," and its invariable recourse to metaphors of the stage, almost on the scale of *Hamlet*. *Macbeth*, my personal favorite among Shakespeare's dramas, always has seemed to me to be set in a Gnostic cosmos, though certainly Shakespeare's own vision is by no means Gnostic in spirit. Gnosticism always manifests a great horror of time, since time will show that one is nothing in oneself, and that one's ambition to be everything in oneself is only an imitation of the Demiurge, the maker of this ruined world.

Why does Shakespeare give us the theatrical trope throughout *Macbeth*, in a universe that is the *kenoma*, the cosmological emptiness of the Gnostic seers? In *Hamlet*, the trope is appropriate, since Claudius governs a play-act kingdom. Clearly, we confront a more desperate theatricality in *Macbeth*, where the cosmos, and not just the kingdom, is an apocalyptic stage, even as it is in *King Lear*. Macbeth's obsession with time is the actor's obsession, and the director's, rather than the poet-playwright's. It is the fear of saying the wrong thing at the wrong time, thus ruining the illusion, which is that one is anything at all.

What always remains troublingly sympathetic about Macbeth is partly that he represents our own Oedipal ambitions, and partly that his opposition to true nature *is* Faustian. Brutally murderous, Macbeth nevertheless is profoundly and engagingly imaginative. He is a visionary Jacobean hero-villain, but unlike Richard III, Iago, and Edmund, and unlike the hero-villains of Webster and Tourneur (Bosola, Flamineo, Ludovico, Vindice), Macbeth takes no pride or pleasure in limning his night-piece and finding it his best. Partly that is because he does not and cannot limn it wholly by himself anyway. Both the supernatural and the natural play a very large part—the witches throughout, and the legitimately natural, almost genealogical revenge of Birnam Wood coming to Dunsinane.

These interventions, demonic and retributive, mean that Macbeth never can get anything quite right, and he is always too cursed with imagination not to know it. Macbeth, far from being the author of that greatest of all night-pieces, *Macbeth*, is merely the object of the drama's force, so much a part of its terrible nature that he needs to augment his crimes steadily just so as to prolong himself in time. ⟨ . . . ⟩

Everything that Macbeth speaks in the course of the drama leads into its most famous and most powerful speech, as fierce a Gnostic declaration as exists in our language:

> To-morrow, and to-morrow, and to-morrow,
> Creeps in this petty pace from day to day,
> To the last syllable of recorded time;
> And all our yesterdays have lighted fools
> The way to dusty death. Out, out, brief candle!
> Life's but a walking shadow, a poor player,
> That struts and frets his hour upon the stage,
> And then is heard no more. It is a tale
> Told by an idiot, full of sound and fury,
> Signifying nothing.

The dramatist, according to Macbeth, is the Demiurge, who destroys all meaning whatsoever. But his nihilistic play, featuring life as hero-villain, is so badly acted in its most crucial part that the petty pace of fallen time is only accentuated. Macbeth therefore ends in total consciousness that he has been thrown into the cosmological emptiness:

> I gin to be a-weary of the sun,
> And wish th' estate o' th' world were now undone.

Mysticism, according to an ancient formulation, fails and then becomes apocalyptic. The apocalyptic fails, and then becomes Gnosticism. Gnosticism, having no hopes for or in this life, necessarily cannot fail. Macbeth, at the close, cannot fail, because he has murdered all hope and all meaning. What he has not murdered is only interest, our interest, our own deep investment in our own inwardness, at all costs, at every cost. Bloody tyrant though he be, Macbeth remains the unsurpassed representation of imagination gone beyond limits, into the abyss of our emptiness.

—Harold Bloom. Introduction to *Macbeth* (New York: Chelsea House Publishers, 1988): pp. 1–2, 4.

Plot Summary of
Antony and Cleopatra

The major part of the play, as often in Shakespeare's works, is contained in the short opening scene (**Act I**, scene one). Mark Antony, one of three triumvirs who rule the Roman Empire (Octavius Caesar and Lepidus are the other two), and Cleopatra, the Queen of Egypt, are infatuated with each other. When the first messenger from Rome comes to call Antony back, Cleopatra mocks him.

In scenes two and three, the tension between Antony's political obligation and his love for Cleopatra increases. More messengers arrive from Rome with bad news: the unrest threatening the triumvirate, forces from Parthia who have conquered Syria, and, last but not least, the death of Antony's wife, Fulvia. Despite Cleopatra's use of all her charm to keep him, Antony is compelled to return home ("I must from this enchanting queen break off.")

As he announces his decision to her, the crisis reaches its climax. Ultimately, Cleopatra accepts his departure as inevitable. Scene four takes place in Rome, where Octavius Caesar, in his conversation with Lepidus, openly disapproves of Antony's conduct. The difference between Caesar and Antony is obvious. The messenger interrupts Caesar to announce the defiance of Pompey.

Scene five shows Cleopatra in Alexandria. She is bored without Antony, and she longs for news of him.

In **Act II**, scene one, Pompey and his allies, the pirates Menecrates and Menas, are introduced. They do not suspect that Antony is on his way to Rome.

Scene two takes place in Rome. Antony faces one crisis after another. After Octavius rigidly accuses Antony, they agree to overlook their differences. Agrippa, a follower of Octavius, proposes that Antony marry Octavia, Octavius' widowed sister, and thus strengthen the ties of friendship. The most trusted of Antony's officers, Enobarbus, pays tribute to Cleopatra at the close of the scene, preparing for Antony's desertion of Octavia.

In scene three, Antony tells Octavia that the world and his duties will divide him from her. In a conversation with a Soothsayer, the audience learns that Antony has made up his mind to go back to Cleopatra: "I will to Egypt;/And though I make this marriage for my peace,/I' th' East my pleasure lies." From this moment Antony's decline begins.

In Act II, scene four, Lepidus, Maecenas, and Agrippa prepare for the meeting with Pompey. Scene five brings us back to Alexandria, to Cleopatra, infuriated with the messenger who has brought her news about Antony's marriage ("The most infectious pestilence upon thee!"). Unlike the audience, Cleopatra does not know that Antony has decided to return to Egypt.

Scene six takes place by the mount of Misena. Pompey and the triumvirs meet, and Pompey unexpectedly accepts the agreement. What is supposed to be a crisis turns into a celebration. The scene closes with Enobarbus' prediction that Antony and Octavius will split, since they lack any mutual grounds to unite them.

In scene seven, the triumvirs meet with Pompey on his galley and celebrate the peace accord. Menas approaches Pompey to suggest that the triumvirs be killed while they are on his ship. Pompey strongly refuses, because "it does not lead to his honour."

Act III begins while the commanders are celebrating. At the same time, in Syria, to the eastern boarder of the Roman empire, Pacorus, the eldest son of Orodes, King of Parthia, has been killed in the battle against Ventidius. The scene shows the heroism of the subordinates.

Scene two presents a cheerful dialogue between Agrippa and Enobarbus about the self-interest and mistrust of the triumvirs. The next scene returns to Alexandria, where Cleopatra is still questioning the same messenger. Scene four takes place in Athens, where we witness Antony's accusations against Octavius Caesar to Octavia. The rift between Antony and Octavius develops swiftly.

From the dialogue between Enobarbus and Eros in Athens, in scene five, the audience learns that Octavius Caesar has dismissed Lepidus from the triumvirate and that Pompey has been murdered. The Roman Empire is now divided between Caesar and Antony.

In scene six, which parallels Act III, scene four, Caesar explains his motives for turning against Antony. The word has reached Rome that Antony has returned to Egypt and has bestowed kingdoms upon Cleopatra's sons. The arrival of Octavia provokes further animosity in Caesar. The battle seems inevitable.

In scene seven, the location is Actium on the northwest coast of Greece. Caesar has declared war against Antony and Cleopatra (or Cleopatra alone, as may be implied by the line "Is't not denounced against us? Why should not we/Be there in person?"). Enobarbus rightly fears that Cleopatra's presence will distract Antony in battle. Antony decides to fight at sea, against Enobarbus' and the soldiers' advice.

Scenes eight, nine, and ten of Act III depict the battle in which thousands of men are involved. The audience finds out what has happened from Enobarbus and Scarus: after Cleopatra and his supporters begin to abandon him,

Antony has fled, following Cleopatra. As the scene closes, Enobarbus contemplates deserting Antony as well.

Defeated, Antony asks to be left alone in scene eleven of Act III. Now he has to bargain with Caesar. When Cleopatra, led by Charmian and Eros, enter, Antony "unqualitied with very shame" says: "I have offended reputation—/A most unnoble swerving."

Act III, scene twelve is located in Caesar's camp outside Alexandria. An ambassador from Antony conveys Antony's request to live either in Egypt or Athens (which Caesar denies) and Cleopatra's wish to have the crown of Ptolomies for her heirs (which will be fulfilled if she drives Antony out or has him put to death.) Caesar's plan is to create a split between them, and he sends Thyreus to win Cleopatra.

In Act III, scene thirteen, the ambassador brings news to Antony. Thyreus flatters Cleopatra. Antony, believing that Cleopatra too has betrayed him, has him whipped. He sends Thyreus back with a defiant message. In the last speech of the scene, Enobarbus finally decides to abandon Antony.

In **Act IV,** scene one, Caesar prepares to fight "the last battle" against Antony. In the next act, Antony takes leave of his servants, warning them that tomorrow they might serve another master. In scene three, Shakespeare creates the mysterious abandonment of Antony's guardian spirit, the god Hercules. (Antony fostered the idea that he was a descendant of Hercules.) Shakespeare conveys a premonition of Antony's defeat to the audience.

Act IV, scene four is a sentimental one, in which Cleopatra is arming Antony in the presence of Eros and Charmian.

Scene five presents the departure of Enobarbus to Caesar.

In scene six Enobarbus enters with Caesar and Agrippa. The difference between the two antipodal characters, Antony and Caesar, is obvious in this scene. Whereas Caesar treats the deserters badly, Antony sends Enobarbus' treasure after him—an act which makes Enobarbus want to die.

In Act IV, scene seven, Antony seems to win a victory, which loyal Scarus joyfully celebrates. Exhilarated, Antony returns to Cleopatra (IV, 8). Trumpets bring the scene to a climax.

Enobarbus dies of a broken heart in scene nine. In scene ten, Caesar prepares to fight by the sea, and Antony sets off to the hillside to watch the clash.

In Act IV, scene twelve, Antony meets disaster when one of his fleet deserts to Caesar's army. He is convinced that Cleopatra has betrayed him and expresses his rage to Scarus, and then to Cleopatra herself. In Act IV, scene thirteen, Cleopatra flees into the tomb ("To th' monument!") and sends a deceitful message to Antony that she has slain herself.

Act IV, scene fourteen shows Antony's rapid decline. At the news of Cleopatra's suicide, Antony asks his only remaining servant, Eros, to kill him. Eros refuses, killing himself instead. Antony attempts to commit suicide; although he strikes a mortal blow, his death is not instantaneous, and his guard refuses to finish the job. Dying, Antony learns that Cleopatra is still alive. (Fearing the effect of her previous message, Cleopatra sent a message with Diomedes.)

In Act IV, scene fifteen, Antony is brought in to Cleopatra. While Antony is trying to deliver his last words, Cleopatra characteristically interrupts him. Finally, he speaks and asks to be remembered by his achievements, not by his end. Cleopatra begins to ponder suicide.

Act V opens at Caesar's camp with the announcement of Antony's death. Caesar denies any responsibility for it. Although he seems to be generous toward Cleopatra, he contrives to take her as a prisoner.

The last scene takes place inside Cleopatra's monument. Cleopatra stays on stage throughout this scene. Caesar fears that she, by committing suicide, can defeat him, and he tries to forestall it by sending his officers (Proculeius, Gallus, soldiers) to guard her. After the encounter with Caesar, who flatters her but cannot come under her spell, Cleopatra sends for the asp and regards suicide as a noble act. When Dollabella confides that Caesar really intends to display her in his triumphal procession in Rome, her will to die is confirmed. She orders her best attire with the words "I am again for Cydnus/To meet Mark Antony" (she met him for the first time in Cydnus). The clown enters with a basket of figs and the "worm of Nilus" (a snake) hidden in it. Cleopatra applies the asp to her breast and dies. She has outwitted Octavius Caesar and she has given her death a transcendental meaning. ✿

List of Characters in
Antony and Cleopatra

Cleopatra is the Queen of Egypt, in love with Antony. She uses all her histrionic devices to keep him away from Rome. Harold Goddard called her the most gifted character Shakespeare ever created. She makes her act of death an act of transcendental beauty.

Antony is one of the triumvirs ("the triple pillars of the world") of the Roman Empire; Asia is his province. Fascinated by Cleopatra, he neglects his political duties and leads a life of pleasure in Egypt. He commits suicide after his defeat by Octavius, after the untrue news of Cleopatra's death has reached him. "A rarer spirit never did steer humanity."

Octavius Caesar is one of the triumvirs at the beginning of the play. He is a political man, the antipode of Antony. At the end of the play, after his victory over Antony at Actium and Alexandria, the entire Roman empire is in his control. Dr. Johnson, though, wrote about Caesar's "heartless littleness."

Lepidus is the third triumvir, who tries to mediate between Octavius and Antony. During the celebration of the peace accord with Pompey, he is carried off drunk. Octavius deprives him of power and imprisons him.

Sextus Pompeius (Pompey) is the son of Pompey the Great, whom Julius Caesar defeated. With the pirates Menas and Menecrates, he has a powerful navy. After the treaty with the triumvirs, we hear that Pompey has been defeated.

Octavia is the sister of Octavius Caesar. She becomes the wife of Antony as part of a political scheme.

Enobarbus is a trusted friend of Antony. He advises Antony to fight on land rather than on the sea (the Battle of Actium). He, however, deserts Antony for Caesar, but he dies of a broken heart when Antony sends all his treasure after him.

Eros is Antony's servant. He has sworn to kill his master if commanded, but when asked to do so, he kills himself instead.

Charmian is a waiting woman to Cleopatra. She applies the asp to her own breast as the guards enter.

Iras is an attendant to Cleopatra. She helps her Queen dress in her "best attire." We do not know how she dies—when Cleopatra bids her farewell, she just falls and dies.

The Soothsayer is an astronomer of Egypt who warns Antony that his spirit will be always overcome by Octavius' when they face each other.

The Clown is a man who brings in a basket with figs and the snake concealed in it. The short episode when he jokes bawdily with Cleopatra before she dies, raises the dramatic tension of Cleopatra's suicide. ✿

Critical Views on
Antony and Cleopatra

JOHN DRYDEN ON CHARACTERIZATION IN THE PLAY

[The English poet, dramatist, and literary critic John Dryden
(1631–1700) so dominated the literary scene of his day that it is
known as the Age of Dryden. His major works are the poem *Annus
Mirabilis* (1667), the heroic tragedy *The Indian Queen* (1664), and
a tragicomedy, *Secret Love, or the Maiden Queen* (1667). His tragedy,
All for Love (1677), is based on Shakespeare's *Antony and Cleopatra*.
This extract, taken from Dryden's preface to the published play, discusses his own characterization in the play.]

The death of *Antony* and *Cleopatra*, is a Subject which has been treated by
the greatest Wits of our Nation, after *Shakespeare;* and by all so variously,
that their example has given me the confidence to try my self in this Bowe of
Ulysses amongst the Crowd of Sutors; and, withal, to take my own measures,
in aiming at the Mark. I doubt not but the same Motive has prevailed with
all of us in this attempt; I mean the excellency of the Moral; for the chief
persons represented, were famous patterns of unlawful love; and their end
accordingly was unfortunate. All reasonable men have long since concluded,
That the Heroe of the Poem, ought not to be a character of perfect Virtue,
for, then, he could not, without injustice, be made unhappy; nor yet altogether wicked, because he could not then be pitied: I have therefore steer'd
the middle course; and have drawn the character of *Antony* as favourably as
Plutarch, Appian, and *Dion Cassius* wou'd give me leave: the like I have observ'd in *Cleopatra.* That which is wanting to work up the pity to a greater
heighth, was not afforded me by the story: for the crimes of love which they
both committed, were not occasion'd by any necessity, or fatal ignorance,
but were wholly voluntary; since our passions are, or ought to be, within our
power. The Fabrick of the Play is regular enough, as to the inferior parts of
it; and the Unities of Time, Place, and Action, more exactly observ'd, than,
perhaps, the *English* Theater requires. Particularly, the Action is so much
one, that it is the only of the kind without Episode, or Underplot; every
Scene in the Tragedy conducing to the main design, and every Act conclud-
ing with a turn of it. The greatest errour in the contrivance seems to be in
the person of *Octavia:* For, though I might use the priviledge of a Poet, to in-
troduce her into *Alexandria,* yet I had not enough consider'd, that the compassion she mov'd to her self and children, was destructive to that which I
reserv'd for *Antony* and *Cleopatra;* whose mutual love being founded upon
vice, must lessen the favour of the Audience to them, when Virtue and Inno-

cence were oppress'd by it. And, though I justified *Antony* in some measure, by making *Octavia's* departure, to proceed wholly from her self; yet the force of the first Machine still remain'd; and the dividing of pity, like the cutting of a River into many Channels, abated the strength of the natural stream. But this is an Objection which none of my Critiques have urg'd against me; and therefore I might have let it pass, if I could have resolv'd to have been partial to my self. The faults my Enemies have found, are rather cavils concerning little, and not essential Decencies; which a Master of the Ceremonies may decide betwixt us. The *French* Poets, I confess, are strict Observers of these Punctilio's: They would not, for example, have suffer'd *Cleopatra* and *Octavia* to have met; or if they had met, there must only have pass'd betwixt them some cold civilities, but no eagerness of repartée, for fear of offending against the greatness of their Characters, and the modesty of their Sex. This Objection I foresaw, and at the same time condemn'd: for I judg'd it both natural and probable, that *Octavia,* proud of her new-gain'd Conquest, would search out *Cleopatra* to triumph over her; and that *Cleopatra,* thus attacqu'd, was not of a spirit to shun the encounter: and 'tis not unlikely, that two exasperated Rivals should use such Satyre as I have put into their mouths; for after all, though the one were a *Roman,* and the other a Queen, they were both Women. 'Tis true, some actions, though natural, are not fit to be represented; and broad obscenities in words, ought in good manners to be avoided: expressions therefore are a modest cloathing of our thoughts, as Breeches and Petticoats are of our bodies. If I have kept my self within the bounds of modesty, all beyond it is but nicety and affectation; which is no more but modest deprav'd into a vice: they betray themselves who are too quick of apprehension in such cases, and leave all reasonable men to imagine worse of them, than of the Poet.

—John Dryden, "Preface" to *All for Love*, 1678.

WILLIAM HAZLETT ON CLEOPATRA'S EXUBERANCE

[William Hazlitt (1778–1830) is an English writer best remembered for his essays. Among his many works are *Lectures on the English Poets* (1818), *Lectures on the English Comic Writers* (1819), and *Liber Amoris,* in which he describes the suffering of a love affair that ended disastrously. In this extract taken from his *Characters of Shakespear's Plays* (1817), Hazlitt speaks about the exuberance of Cleopatra's character.]

Cleopatra's whole character is the triumph of the voluptuous, of the love of pleasure and the power of giving it, over every other consideration. Octavia is a dull foil to her, and Fulvia a shrew and shrill-tongued. What a picture do those lines give of her—

> "Age cannot wither her, nor custom steal
> Her infinite variety. Other women cloy
> The appetites they feed, but she makes hungry
> Where most she satisfies."

What a spirit and fire in her conversation with Antony's messenger who brings her the unwelcome news of his marriage with Octavia! How all the pride of beauty and of high rank breaks out in her promised reward to him—

> —————"There's gold, and here
> My bluest veins to kiss!"—

She had great and unpardonable faults, but the grandeur of her death almost redeems them. She learns from the depth of despair the strength of her affections. She keeps her queen-like state in the last disgrace, and her sense of the pleasurable in the last moments of her life. She tastes a luxury in death. After applying the asp, she says with fondness—

> "Dost thou not see my baby at my breast,
> That sucks the nurse asleep?
> As sweet as balm, as soft as air, as gentle.
> Oh Antony!" ⟨ . . . ⟩

The latter scenes of ANTONY AND CLEOPATRA are full of the changes of accident and passion. Success and defeat follow one another with startling rapidity. Fortune sits upon her wheel more blind and giddy than usual. This precarious state and the approaching dissolution of his greatness are strikingly displayed in the dialogue of Antony with Eros.

> "*Antony.* Eros, thou yet behold'st me?
> *Eros.* Ay, noble lord.
> *Antony.* Sometime we see a cloud that's dragonish,
> A vapour sometime, like a bear or lion,
> A towered citadel, a pendant rock,
> A forked mountain, or blue promontory
> With trees upon't, that nod unto the world
> And mock our eyes with air. Thou hast seen these signs,
> They are black vesper's pageants.
> *Eros.* Ay, my lord.
> *Antony.* That which is now a horse, even with a thought
> The rack dislimns, and makes it indistinct
> As water is in water.
> *Eros.* It does, my lord.
> *Antony.* My good knave, Eros, now thy captain is
> Even such a body," &c.

This is, without doubt, one of the finest pieces of poetry in Shakespear. The splendour of the imagery, the semblance of reality, the lofty range of picturesque objects hanging over the world, their evanescent nature, the total uncertainty of what is left behind, are just like the mouldering schemes of human greatness. It is finer than Cleopatra's passionate lamentation over his fallen grandeur, because it is more dim, unstable, unsubstantial. Antony's headstrong presumption and infatuated determination to yield to Cleopatra's wishes to fight by sea instead of land, meet a merited punishment; and the extravagance of his resolutions, increasing with the desperateness of his circumstances, is well commented upon by Œnobarbus.

> —————"I see men's judgments are
> A parcel of their fortunes, and things outward
> Do draw the inward quality after them
> To suffer all alike."

The repentance of Œnobarbus after his treachery to his master is the most affecting part of the play. He cannot recover from the blow which Antony's generosity gives him, and he dies broken-hearted, "a master-leaver and a fugitive."

Shakespear's genius has spread over the whole play a richness like the overflowing of the Nile.

—William Hazlitt, *Characters of Shakespear's Plays* (London: Macmillan and Co., 1817): pp. 60–61, 62–63.

SAMUEL TAYLOR COLERIDGE ON CLEOPATRA'S CHARACTER

[In addition to being one of the greatest British poets of the early nineteenth century, Samuel Taylor Coleridge (1772–1834) was also a penetrating critic. His most famous critical work is *Biographia Literaria* (1817). In 1819 he delivered a series of lectures on Shakespeare, which were published posthumously in his *Literary Remains* (1836–39). In this extract from that work, he comments on Cleopatra's character.]

This play (*Antony and Cleopatra*) should be perused in mental contrast with *Romeo and Juliet*;—as the love of passion and appetite opposed to the love of affection and instinct. But the art displayed in the character of Cleopatra is profound; in this, especially, that the sense of criminality in her passion is lessened by our insight into its depth and energy, at the very moment that we cannot but perceive that the passion itself springs out of the habitual craving of a licentious nature, and that it is supported and reinforced by voluntary stimulus and sought-for associations, instead of blossoming out of spontaneous emotion.

—Samuel Taylor Coleridge, *"Antony and Cleopatra"* [1819], *Literary Remains*, vol. 2, edited by Henry Nelson Coleridge (London: Pickering, 1836): p. 143.

George Bernard Shaw on the Battle of Actium

[George Bernard Shaw (1856–1950) was an Irish dramatist and literary critic. Among his most famous plays are *The Devil's Disciple* (1897), *Caesar and Cleopatra* (1901), *Man and Superman* (1905), *Pygmalion* (1913; adapted into the popular musical and motion picture *My Fair Lady*), and *Saint Joan* (1923). Although he won the Nobel Prize for Literature in 1925, he refused the award. This extract is taken from Shaw's writings on the plays of Shakespeare. Here Shaw objects to Shakespeare's presentation of the battle of Actium.]

Shakespear's *Antony* and *Cleopatra* must needs be as intolerable to the true Puritan as it is vaguely distressing to the ordinary healthy citizen, because, after giving a faithful picture of the soldier broken down by debauchery, and the typical wanton in whose arms such men perish, Shakespear finally strains all his huge command of rhetoric and stage pathos to give a theatrical sublimity to the wretched end of the business, and to persuade foolish spectators that the world was well lost by the twain. Such falsehood is not to be borne except by the real Cleopatras and Antonys (they are to be found in every public house) who would no doubt be glad enough to be transfigured by some poet as immortal lovers. Woe to the poet who stoops to such folly! The lot of the man who sees life truly and thinks about it romantically is Despair. How well we know the cries of that despair! Vanity of vanities, all is vanity! moans the Preacher, when life has at last taught him that Nature will not dance to his moralist-made tunes. Thackeray, scores of centuries later, was still baying the moon in the same terms. Out, out, brief candle! cries Shakespear, in his tragedy of the modern literary man as murderer and witch consulter. Surely the time is past for patience with writers who, having to choose between giving up life in despair and discarding the trumpery moral kitchen scales in which they try to weigh the universe, superstitiously stick to the scales, and spend the rest of the lives they pretend to despise in breaking men's spirits. But even in pessimism there is a choice between intellectual honesty and dishonesty. Hogarth drew the rake and the harlot without glorifying their end. Swift, accepting our system of morals and religion, delivered the inevitable verdict of that system on us through the mouth of the king of Brobdingnag, and described Man as the Yahoo, shocking his superior the horse by his every action. Strindberg, the only genuinely Shakespearean modern dramatist, shews that the female Yahoo, measured by romantic standards, is viler than her male dupe and slave. I respect these resolute tragi-comedians: they are logical and faithful: they force you to face the fact that you must either accept their conclusions as valid (in which case it is cowardly to continue living) or admit that their way of judging conduct is absurd. But when your Shakespears and Thackerays huddle up the matter at the end by killing somebody and covering your eyes with the undertaker's handkerchief, duly onioned with some pathetic phrase, as The flight of angels sing thee to thy rest, or Adsum, or the like, I have no respect for them at all: such maudlin tricks may impose on tea-drunkards, not on me.

Besides, I have a technical objection to making sexual infatuation a tragic theme. Experience proves that it is only effective in the comic spirit. We can bear to see Mrs Quickly pawning her plate for love of Falstaff, but not Antony running away from the battle of Actium for love of Cleopatra. Let realism have its demonstration, comedy its criticism, or even bawdry its horselaugh at the expense of sexual infatuation, if it must; but to ask us to subject our souls to its ruinous glamor, to worship it, deify it, and imply that it alone makes our life worth living, is nothing but folly gone mad erotically—a thing compared to which Falstaff's unbeglamored drinking and drabbing is respectable and rightminded. Whoever, then, expects to find Cleopatra a Circe and Caesar a hog in these pages, had better lay down my book and be spared a disappointment.

—George Bernard Shaw, "Better than Shakespear?" [1900], *Three Plays for Puritans* (1901; reprinted London: Constable, 1930): pp. xxx—xxxii.

HAROLD C. GODDARD ON THE CHARACTERS OF ANTONY AND CLEOPATRA

[Harold C. Goddard (1878–1950) was for many years head of the English department at Swarthmore College. He was the author of *Studies in New England Transcendentalism* (1906) and the editor of an edition of Ralph Waldo Emerson's essays (1926). One of the most important books on Shakespeare is Goddard's *The Meaning of Shakespeare,* published the year after his death. In this extract Goddard comments on the characters of Cleopatra and Antony.]

It is not by chance that Shakespeare puts the description of the meeting of Antony and Cleopatra at Cydnus right after the account of the selling of his sister by Octavius to Antony. Caesar issues his orders and Octavia obeys. Cleopatra does not have to issue orders. The winds fall in love with the very sails of the barge she sits in. The water is amorous of its oars and follows faster. Boys and maids, like Cupids and Nereides, fan and tend her. The city pours out its multitudes to behold her. But for the gap it would have left in nature, the air itself would have gone to gaze on her.

> I saw her once,

says Enobarbus,

> Hop forty paces through the public street;
> And having lost her breath, she spoke, and panted,
> That she did make defect perfection
> And, breathless, power breathe forth.

Here is power of another species than power military or political. Cleopatra's beauty may have been more the Dionysian beauty of vitality than the Apollonian beauty of form, but whatever it was it justifies Keat's dictum:

> 'tis the eternal law
> That first in beauty should be first in might.

And yet the magnetism that emanates from her at her first meeting with Antony at Cydnus is mere witchcraft and magic compared with the authentic "fire and air" that descends on her before her second immortal meeting with him at the end.

It is this magic and witchcraft that captivate Antony in the first place.

> I must from this enchanting queen break off.

The adjective shows that it is with the semi-mythological Cleopatra, the ancestral image of Woman she evokes within him, the gypsy, Egypt, the Serpent of old Nile, that he is in love. The fascination is mutual, and she in turn endows him with superhuman attributes. He is anything to her from the demi-Atlas of the Earth to Mars. The tradition that Antony was descended from Hercules, son of Zeus, abets this cosmic overvaluation of the human being, as does, for him, her assumption of the role of the goddess Isis. In so far as these things amount to a conscious affectation or attribution of divinity—and, even more, a willingness to make political use of them—they degrade the pair deeply in our estimations, proving them victims not only of infatuation with each other but of a self-infatuation far less excusable. But infatuation, analyzed, generally turns out to be more a failure to locate the origin of compelling forces from underneath or from overhead than mere vanity, folly, or egotism in the usual sense. "No man", says Robert Henri, "ever overappreciated a human being." And so when Cleopatra, about to part from Antony, exclaims,

> Eternity was in our lips and eyes,
> Bliss in our brows bent; none our parts so poor
> But was a race of heaven,

it strikes us less as affectation of divinity than as genuine perception of the divine element in love—insight into the heart of something which their wildest words about each other are abortive or rapturous attempts to express. In such poetry as Cleopatra attains in those three lines the illusion becomes almost indistinguishable from the truth. ⟨ . . . ⟩

What wonder that ⟨Antony⟩ cries, when he realizes what he has done:

> Hark! the land bids me tread no more upon't!
> It is asham'd to bear me. . . .
> CLEO.:　　　　O, my lord, my lord,
> Forgive my fearful sails! I little thought
> You would have follow'd.
> ANT.:　　　　Egypt, thou knew'st too well
> My heart was to thy rudder tied by the strings,
> And thou shouldst tow me after. O'er my spirit
> Thy full supremacy thou knew'st, and that
> Thy beck might from the bidding of the gods
> Command me.

But the shame is not the whole story. Even here Shakespeare seems less interested in the outcome of the Battle of Actium than in the nature of that force that at the height of the action can obliterate utterly in the mind of this greatest soldier of the world all thought of military conquest and glory, all concern for what the world will think of his disgrace. Here is a mystery indeed. In the Battle of Actium, war and love—or at least war and something akin to love—grapple, and war wins. Yet does it win? To deepen the enigma the poet proceeds to show that it is precisely out of the dishonor and defeat that the spiritual triumph emerges which is always found at the heart of the highest tragedy. More and more as it nears its end, *Antony and Cleopatra* seems to recede from mere history into myth, or, if you will, to open out and mount above history into a cosmic sunset of imagination.

—Harold C. Goddard, *The Meaning of Shakespeare* (Chicago: University of Chicago Press, 1951): pp. 195–197.

[Anne Barton is Professor of English at Cambridge University, and fellow of Trinity College, Cambridge. She is the author of *Shakespeare and Idea of the Play* and *Ben Jonson, Dramatist.* In this extract Barton discusses Cleopatra's and Antony's complexity.]

Shakespeare, of course, greatly complicated the situation by transferring this moral ambiguity to Antony and Cleopatra themselves. As characters, they become singularly hard to assess or know. Part of their opacity springs from the fact that she has nothing even resembling a soliloquy until the last scene of the play and that Antony is not much more forthcoming about his private intentions. This reticence contrasts sharply not only with the inveterate mental unburdenings of the protagonists in Daniel or Garnier, but with Shakespeare's own, earlier tragic practice. Emrys Jones has argued, in *Scenic Form in Shakespeare,* that the construction of *Antony and Cleopatra*—the wasteful, drifting movement of all those short scenes—reflects the haphazard nature of phenomenal experience, that it seems more like the life process itself than like formal tragedy. I think that this is true, and that the effect is one that Shakespeare reinforces through his handling of the protagonists. With Romeo and Juliet before, with Othello and Desdemona, even with Macbeth and his wife, evaluation of the two individuals concerned and of their relationship had not only been encouraged: it was possible. With Cleopatra and Antony, on the other hand, it simply cannot be managed. They are as mysterious and contradictory as people known in real life. Our place of vantage is basically that of Charmian and Enobarbus: people sufficiently close to their social superiors to witness informal and often undignified behaviour, without participating in motive and reflection like the confidantes in Garnier or Jodelle. It is true that we see more of the picture in range, if not in depth, than these attendant characters. They cannot move, as we can, from Rome to Egypt and back again within an instant, nor are they present in all the scenes. Our perspective upon the affairs of Antony and his mistress is wider than theirs, but this very breadth makes judgment more instead of less difficult.

In this tragedy, other characters are continually trying to describe Cleopatra and Antony, to fix their essential qualities in words. This impulse generates several of the great, set speeches of the play: Enobarbus's description of Cleopatra at Cydnus, or Caesar's account of Antony crossing the Alps, like a lean stag inured to privation. It also makes itself felt in less obvious ways. Because of the constant shifting of scene, the protagonists are forever being discussed by bewildered rivals or subordinates while they themselves are away in Egypt or in Rome. The results of this unremitting attempt at evaluation are bewildering. In the course of the tragedy, Antony is called "the noble Antony," the "courteous Antony," the "firm Roman," "Mars," a "mine of bounty," the "triple pillar of the world," "the demi-atlas of this earth," the "lord of lords, of infinite virtue," the "crown o' the earth," and "the garland of the war." These are only a few of the celebratory epithets. He is also "poor Antony," a "libertine," "the abstract of all faults that all men follow," a "gorgon," a "sworder," an "old ruffian," a "doting mallard," the "ne'er lust-wearied Antony" and a "strumpet's fool." There is no progression among these epithets, no sense of alteration in Antony's character during the play as there is, for instance, with Macbeth. Macbeth begins his tragedy as "worthy Macbeth" and ends it as "this dead butcher." The space between the two descriptions is that of his tragic development. Antony, on the other hand, is all the contradictory things that people say he is more or less simultaneously. Nor is there any neat division of the celebratory and the pejorative between Antony's friends and Antony's enemies. Enobarbus and Octavius are alike in acknowledging both sides of the moon: the bright as well as the dark.

Cleopatra's situation is similar. She is "great Egypt," "dearest queen," a "rare Egyptian," a "triumphant lady," "Thetis," "this great fairy," "day o' the world," "nightingale," "eastern star," a "most sovereign creature," a "lass unparallel'd"—but also a "foul Egyptian," the "false soul of Egypt," a "witch," a "gipsy," a "strumpet," a "whore," a "trull," "salt Cleopatra," a "boggler," a "morsel cold upon dead Caesar's trencher," Antony's "Egyptian dish," the "ribaudred nag of Egypt," and "a cow in June." One may begin to feel that language used so indiscriminately to describe a single personality becomes meaningless and self-defeating, that one would do better to adopt Antony's method when he described a different serpent of old Nile to the drunken Lepidus. "What maner o' thing is your crocodile?" And Antony replies:

> It is shap'd, sir, like itself, and it is as
> broad as it hath breadth: it is just so high
> as it is, and moves with its own organs. It
> lives by that which nourishes it, and the
> elements once out of it, it transmigrates.

It's of its own colour too, and the tears of it—like Cleopatra's—are wet.

> —Anne Barton. "Nature's Piece 'Gainst Fancy': The Divided Catastrophe in *Antony and Cleopatra*." From *An Inaugural Lecture* (unpublished; presented to the Hildred Carlile Chair of English Literature in the University of London tenable at Bedford College, October 1972).

[Harold Bloom, the editor of this series, is Sterling Professor of the Humanities at Yale University and Berg Professor of English at New York University. He is the author of more than 20 books and the editor of over 40 anthologies of both literature and literary criticism. His latest book, *Shakespeare: the Invention of the Human,* was published in November 1998. In this extract, taken from the introduction to a critical anthology on *Antony and Cleopatra* in the Chelsea House series MODERN CRITICAL INTERPRETATIONS, Bloom comments on the grandeur and the sublimity of the title characters' deaths.]

From act 4, scene 14, through to the end of the play, we hear something wonderfully original even for Shakespeare, a great dying fall, the release of a new music. It begins with the dialogue between Antony and his marvelously named, devoted follower, Eros ⟨ . . . ⟩

There is a deliberate touch of the cloud-watching Hamlet in Antony here, but with Hamlet's parodistic savagery modulated into a gentleness that befits the transmutation of the charismatic hero into a self-transcendent consciousness, almost beyond the consolations of farewell. The grandeur of this transformation is enhanced when Antony receives the false tidings Cleopatra sends of her supposed death, with his name her last utterance:

> Unarm, Eros, the long day's task is done,
> And we must sleep.

The answering chorus to that splendor is Cleopatra's, when he dies in her arms:

> The crown o'th'earth doth melt. My lord!
> O, wither'd is the garland of the war,
> The soldier's pole is fall'n! Young boys and girls
> Are level now with men; the odds is gone,
> And there is nothing left remarkable
> Beneath the visiting moon.

Antony touches the Sublime as he prepares to die, but Cleopatra's lament for a lost Sublime is the prelude to a greater sublimity, which is to be wholly her own. She is herself a great actress, so that the difficulty in playing her, for any actress, is quite extraordinary. And though she certainly loved Antony, it is inevitable that, like any great actress, she must love herself all but apocalyptically. Antony has a largeness about him surpassing any other Shakespearean hero except for Hamlet; he is an ultimate version of the charismatic leader, loved and followed because his palpable glory can be shared, in some degree, since he is also magnificently generous. But Shakespeare shrewdly ends him with one whole act of the play to go, and retrospectively we see that the drama is as much Cleopatra's as the two parts of *Henry IV* are Falstaff's.

Remarkable as Antony is in himself, he interests us primarily because he has the splendor that makes him as much a catastrophe for Cleopatra as she is for him. Cleopatra is in love with his exuberance, with the preternatural vitality that impresses even Octavian. But she knows, as we do, that Antony lacks her infinite variety. Their love, in Freudian terms, is not narcissistic but anaclitic; they are propped upon one another, cosmological beings who are likely to be bored by anyone else, by any personality neither their own nor one another's. Antony is Cleopatra's only true match and yet he is not her equal, which may be the most crucial or deepest meaning of the play. An imaginative being in that he moves the imagination of others, he is simply not an imaginer of her stature. He need not play himself; he is Herculean. Cleopatra ceases to play herself only when she is transmuted by his death and its aftermath, and we cannot be sure, even then, that she is not both performing and simultaneously becoming that more transcendent self. Strangely like the dying Hamlet in this single respect, she suggests, at the end, that she stands upon a new threshold of being:

> I am fire and air; my other elements
> I give to baser life.

Is she no longer the earth of Egypt, or the water of the Nile? We have not exactly thought of her as a devoted mother, despite her children by Julius Caesar and by Antony, but in her dying dialogue with Charmian she transmutes the asps, first into her baby, and then apparently into an Antony she might have brought to birth, as in some sense indeed she did:

> CHARMIAN. O eastern star!
> CLEOPATRA.   Peace, peace!
>   Dost thou not see my baby at my breast,
>   That sucks the nurse asleep?
> CHARMIAN.   O, break! O, break!
> CLEOPATRA. As sweet as balm, as soft as air, as gentle—O
>   Antony!—Nay, I will take thee too:
>   [*Applying another asp to her arm.*]
>   What should I stay—   *Dies.*

As Lear dies, Kent cries out "Break, heart, I prithee break!" even as Charmian does here, not wishing upon the rack of this tough world to stretch Cleopatra out longer. When Antony's men find him wounded to death, they lament that "the star is fall'n," and that "time is at his period." Charmian's "O eastern star!" associates one dying lover with the other, even as her echo of Kent suggests that the dying Empress of the East is in something like the innocence of Lear's madness. Cleopatra is sucked to sleep as a mother is by a child, or a woman by a lover, and dies in such peace that Octavian, of all men, is moved to the ultimate tribute:

she looks like sleep,
As she would catch another Antony
In her strong toil of grace.

Bewildering us by her final manifestation of her infinite variety, Cleopatra dies into a beyond, a Sublime where actress never trod.

—Harold Bloom, Introduction to *Antony and Cleopatra* (New York: Chelsea House Publishers, 1988): pp. 2–4. ❀

Works by Shakespeare

Venus and Adonis.	1593
The Rape of Lucrece.	1594
Henry VI.	1594
Titus Andronicus.	1594
The Taming of the Shrew.	1594
Romeo and Juliet.	1597
Richard III.	1597
Richard II.	1597
Love's Labour's Lost.	1598
Henry IV.	1598
The Passionate Pilgrim.	1599
A Midsummer Night's Dream.	1600
The Merchant of Venice.	1600
Much Ado About Nothing.	1600
Henry V.	1600
The Phoenix and the Turtle.	1601
The Merry Wives of Windsor.	1602
Hamlet.	1603
King Lear.	1608
Troilus and Cressida.	1609
Sonnets.	1609
Pericles.	1609

Othello	1622
Mr. William Shakespeares Comedies, Histories & *Tragedies.* ed. John Heminge and Henry Condell.	1623 (First Folio) 1632 (Second Folio) 1663 (Third Folio) 1685 (Fourth Folio).
Poems.	1640
Works. ed. Nicholas Rowe, 6 vols.	1709
Works. ed. Alexander Pope, 6 vols.	1723–25
Works. ed. Lewis Theobald, 7 vols.	1733
Works. ed. Thomas Hanmer, 6 vols.	1743–144
Works. ed. William Warburton, 8 vols.	1747
Plays. ed. Samuel Johnson, 8 vols.	1765
Plays and Poems. ed. Edmond Malone, 10 vols.	1790
The Family Shakespeare. ed. Thomas Bowdler, 4 vols.	1807
Works. ed. J. Payne Collier, 8 vols.	1842–44
Works. ed. H. N. Hudson, 11 vols.	1851–56
Works. ed. Alexander Dyce, 6 vols.	1857
Works. ed. Richard Grant White, 12 vols.	1857–66
Works (Cambridge Edition). ed. William George Clark, John Glover, and William Aldis Wright, 9 vols.	1863–66
A New Variorum Edition of the Works of Shakespeare. ed. H. H. Furness et al.	1871

Works. ed. W. J. Rolfe, 40 vols.	1871–96
The Pitt Press Shakespeare. ed. A. W. Verity, 13 vols.	1890–1905
The Warwick Shakespeare, 13 vols.	1893–1938
The Temple Shakespeare. ed. Israel Gollancz, 40 vols.	1894–97
The Arden Shakespeare. Ed W. J. Craig, R. H. Case et al, 37 vols.	1899–1924
The Shakespeare Apocrypha. ed. C. F. Tucker Brooke.	1908
The Yale Shakespeare. ed. Wilbur L. Cross, Tucker Brooke, and Willard Highley Durham, 40 vols.	1912–27
The New Shakespeare (Cambridge Edition). ed., 38 vols. Arthur Quiller-Couch and John Dover Wilson.	1921–62
The New Temple Shakespeare. ed. M. R. Ridley, 39 vols.	1934–36
Works. ed. George Lyman Kittredge.	1936
The Penguin Shakespeare. ed. G. B. Harrison, 36 vols.	1937–59
The New Clarendon Shakespeare. ed. R. E. C. Houghton.	1938–
The Arden Shakespeare. ed. Una Ellis-Fermor et al.	1951–
The Complete Pelican Shakespeare. ed. Alfred Harbage.	1969
The Complete Signet Classic Shakespeare. ed. Sylvan Barnet.	1972
The Oxford Shakespeare. ed. Stanley Wells.	1982–
The New Cambridge Shakespeare. ed. Philip Brockbank.	1984–

Works about
Shakespeare's Tragedies

Bayley, John. *Shakespeare and Tragedy*. London: Routledge & Kegan Paul, 1981.

Barber, C. L., and Richard P. Wheeler. *The Whole Journey: Shakespeare's Power of Development*. Berkeley: University of California Press, 1986.

Barton, Anne. *Shakespeare and the Idea of the Play*. London: Chatto & Windus, 1961.

Bloom, Harold, ed. *William Shakespeare's Othello*. New York: Chelsea House, 1987

————. *William Shakespeare's King Lear*. New York: Chelsea House, 1987.

Bonnefoy, Yves. "Readiness, Ripeness: *Hamlet, Lear.*" Trans. John T. Mc-Naughton, *New Literary History* 17, No. 3 (Spring 1986): 485–91.

Booth, Wayne C. "Macbeth as Tragic Hero." *Journal of General Education* 6, No. 1 (October 1951): 17–25.

Burke, Kenneth. "*Othello:* An Essay to Illustrate a Method." *Hudson Review* 4 (1951–52): 165–203.

Calderwood, James L. *If It Were Done: Macbeth and Tragic Action*. Amherst: University of Massachusetts Press, 1986.

Cohen, Derek. *Shakespearean Motives*. New York: St. Martin's Press, 1988.

Croce, Benedetto. *Ariosto, Shakespeare and Cornelle*. New York : Henry Holt & Co., 1920.

Empson, William. "Hamlet When New." *Sewanee Review* 61 (1953): 15–42, 185–205.

————. *Essays on Shakespeare*. ed. David B. Pirie. Cambridge: Cambridge University Press, 1986.

Everett, Barbara. "The New *King Lear.*" *Critical Quarterly* 2, No. 4 (Winter 1960): 325–39.

————. "Reflections on the Sentimentalist's *Othello.*" *Critical Quarterly* 3 (1961): 127–39.

Felperin, Howard. *Shakespearean Representation.* Princeton: Princeton University Press, 1977.

Fineman, Joel. "The Sound of *O* in *Othello:* The Real of the Tragedy of Desire." In *The Subjectivity Effect in Western Literary Tradition: Essays toward the Release of Shakespeare's Will.* Cambridge, Mass: MIT Press, 1991.

Frye, Northrop. *Fools of Time: Studies in Shakespeare Tragedy.* Toronto: University of Toronto Press, 1967.

Girard, René. "Hamlet's Dull Revenge." In *Literary Theory/Renaissance Texts,* ed. Patricia Parker and David Quint. Baltimore: John Hopkins University Press, 1986.

———. *A Theater of Envy: William Shakespeare.* New York: Oxford University Press, 1991.

Hecht, Anthony. *Obliggati.* New York: Athenaeum, 1986, pp. 51–84.

Kermode, Frank. *Shakespeare, Spencer, Donne.* London: Routledge & Kegan Paul, 1971.

Kirsch, Arthur. "The Emotional Landscape of *King Lear.*" *Shakespeare Quarterly* 39, No. 2 (Summer 1988): 154–70.

Knight, W. G. *The Wheel of Fire.* Oxford: Oxford University Press: 1930.

———. *The Imperial Theme.* 3rd edition, London: Methuen, 1951.

Knights, L. C. *An Approach to Hamlet.* London: Chatto & Windus, 1960.

———. *Some Shakespearean Themes.* London: Chatto & Windus, 1959.

———. *Hamlet and Other Shakespearean Essays.* Cambridge: Cambridge University Press, 1979.

Mack, Maynard Jr. *Killing the King: Three Studies in Shakespeare's Tragic Structure.* New Haven: Yale University Press, 1973.

McAlindon, T. *Shakespeare's Tragic Cosmos.* Cambridge: Cambridge University Press, 1991.

Muir, Kenneth. *Shakespeare's Tragic Sequence.* London: Hutchinson University Library, 1972.

Nevo, Ruth. *Tragic Form in Shakespeare.* Princeton: Princeton University Press, 1972.

Nutall, A. D. *A New Mimesis: Shakespeare and Representation of Reality.* London: Methuen, 1983.

Rosen, William. *Shakespeare and the Craft of Tragedy.* Cambridge, Mass: Harvard University Press, 1960.

Sanders, Wilbur. *The Dramatist and the Received Idea: Studies in the Plays of Marlowe and Shakespeare.* Cambridge: Cambridge University Press, 1968.

Spuregeon, Caroline F. E. *Shakespeare's Imagery and What It Tells Us.* Cambridge: Cambridge University Press, 1935.

Stoll, Elmer Edgar. *Shakespeare and Other Masters.* Cambridge, Mass: Harvard University Press, 1940.

University of Dayton Review 14, No. 1 (Winter 1979–80). Special *Macbeth* issue.

Wilson, Harold S. *On the Design of Shakespearean Tragedy.* Toronto: University of Toronto Press, 1957.

Index of
Themes and Ideas

ANTONY AND CLEOPATRA, 13, 92–110; Agrippa in, 92, 93, 94; Mark Antony in, 11, 92, 93–94, 95, 96, 99, 100, 101, 103, 104–10; Bloom on deaths of Antony and Cleopatra in, 108–10; Octavius Caesar in, 92, 93, 94, 95, 96, 104, 106, 109; characters in, 96; Charmian in, 94, 96, 106, 109; Cleopatra in, 11, 92–93, 94, 95, 96, 99–102, 103, 104–10; Clown in, 97; Coleridge on Cleopatra's character in, 101–2; critical views on, 9, 10, 11, 98–110; Dryden on characterization in, 98–99; Enobarbus in, 92, 93, 94, 96, 101, 106, 107; Eros in, 93, 94, 95, 96, 100, 108; Fulvia in, 92, 100; Goddard on Antony and Cleopatra in, 103–5; Hazlitt on Cleopatra's exuberance in, 99–101; Iras in, 96; Lepidus in, 92, 93, 96, 107; Maecenas in, 92; Menas in, 92, 93; Menecrates in, 92; Octavia in, 93, 96, 98, 99, 100, 104, 107; plot summary of, 92–95; Sextus Pompeius (Pompey) in, 92, 93, 96; Shaw on battle of Actium in, 102–3; Soothsayer in, 92, 97

HAMLET, 13, 15–32; Brandes on *Macbeth* compared with, 79–82; characters in, 19–20; Claudius in, 10, 15, 16–17, 18, 19, 21, 26, 48; Coleridge on *Macbeth* compared with, 78–79; critical views on, 9–10, 21–32, 43, 71, 78–82; Fortinbras in, 15, 16, 17, 18, 20; Freud on Hamlet's deepest impulses in, 28–30; Gertrude in, 10, 15, 16, 17, 18, 19, 48; Goddard on Hamlet's hesitation in, 30–32; Goethe's Meister's fascination with Hamlet in, 22–24; Hamlet in, 9–10, 15–16, 17, 18, 19, 21–32, 66, 80–81, 82–83, 108; Hazlitt on Hamlet's power of action in, 26–27; Horatio in, 15, 17, 18, 19; Johnson on Hamlet's variety in, 21–22; Laertes in, 15, 18, 20, 21, 32; Nietzsche on Hamlet's Dionysiac traits in, 28; Old Hamlet in, 15–16, 17, 19, 25, 32; Ophelia in, 15, 16, 17, 18, 19, 21, 22, 25, 29, 32; plot summary of, 15–18; Polonius in, 15, 16–17, 19, 25, 26, 31, 32; as radical theatrical experiment, 9; Rosencrantz and Guildenstern in, 16, 17, 18, 20, 25, 26; Schlegel on Hamlet's flaws in, 24–25

KING LEAR, 13, 53–72; Duke of Albany in, 53, 54, 55, 56, 57, 68, 72; audience of like Lear, 68–70; Bradley on Lear's insanity in, 66–68; characters in, 57–58; contraries in, 10; Cordelia in, 53, 54, 55, 56, 57, 59–60, 61, 63, 65, 66, 70, 71, 72; Earl of Cornwall in, 53–54, 55, 56, 57, 68, 71, 72; critical views on, 9, 10, 41, 43, 59–72; Edgar in, 53, 54, 55–56, 58, 63, 65, 69, 70–72; Edgar's biblical echoes in, 70–72;

Edmund in, 43, 51, 53, 54, 55, 56, 58, 60, 63, 65, 69, 71, 90; Fool in, 53, 54, 58, 65, 72; Earl of Gloucester in, 53, 54, 55, 56, 57, 59–60, 63, 69, 70, 71–72; Goneril in, 51, 53, 54, 55, 56, 57, 63, 69, 71; Hazlitt on logic of passion in, 62–64; Johnson on Cordelia's death in, 59–60; Earl of Kent in, 53, 54, 55, 56, 57–58, 63, 65, 69–70, 71, 72, 109; Lamb on as play beyond all art, 61–62; King Lear in, 10, 53, 54, 55, 56, 57, 59, 61, 62–63, 64, 65, 66, 70, 71, 109; Leontes in, 43; Oswald in, 53, 54, 55, 56, 58; plot summary of, 53–56; Regan in, 51, 53–54, 55, 56, 57, 63, 69, 71

MACBETH, 13, 73–91; Banquo in, 73, 74, 75, 77, 87; Bloom on Macbeth's gnostic declarations in, 89–91; Bradley on Macbeth's imagination in, 82–84; Brandes on *Hamlet* compared with, 79–82; characters in, 77; Coleridge on *Hamlet* compared with, 78–79; critical views on, 9, 10, 30, 43, 52, 71, 78–91; Donalbain in, 73, 74; Duncan in, 73, 74, 77, 83, 87; Fleance in, 73, 74, 77; *Hamlet* compared with, 78–82; Johnson on realism in, 78; lack of punning in, 78–79; Lenox in, 74, 75; Macbeth in, 10, 45, 48, 65, 73, 74–75, 76, 77, 78, 79, 80–81, 82–86, 87, 88, 89–91, 107; Macbeth's destruction in, 84–86; Lady Macbeth in, 73, 74–75, 77, 78, 82, 83, 87, 89; Macduff in, 74, 75, 76, 77, 88, 89; Lady Macduff in, 88; Malcolm in, 73, 74, 75, 76, 77, 88; Old Man in, 74; plot summary of, 73–76; Ross in, 75; two marriages in, 86–89; The Witches/Weird Sisters in, 73, 75, 77, 80

OTHELLO, 13, 33–52; Auden on Iago as practical joker in, 47–51; Bianca in, 35, 36, 37; Bloom on Iago's manipulations in, 51–52; Brabantio in, 33, 36, 37; Bradley on distinguished characteristics of, 41–44; Cassio in, 33, 34, 35, 36, 37; characters in, 37; Clown in, 46–47; critical views on, 9, 10, 38–52, 64; Desdemona in, 33–34, 35, 36, 37, 38, 39, 40, 42–43, 44, 47, 48, 51, 65, 66; Desdemona's suffering in, 42–43; as drama of modern life, 43–44; Emilia in, 10, 33, 34, 35, 36, 37, 51–52; Empson on good and evil in, 44–46; Goddard on inaudible music in, 46–47; Grantiano in, 36, 37; Hazlitt on Othello's mind in, 38–40; Iago in, 10, 33–34, 35, 36, 37, 38–40, 41, 42, 43–44, 44, 45–46, 47–52, 65, 82, 90; intrigue in, 43; jealousy in, 42; Johnson on Iago's character in, 38; Lodovico in, 35, 36, 37; method of construction of, 42; Montano in, 34, 36, 37, 47; plot summary of, 33–36; Roderigo in, 33, 34, 35, 36, 37; Shaw on Iago's complex character in, 40–41; Duke of Venice in, 33, 35, 37

SHAKESPEARE, WILLIAM: biography of, 12–14; Tolstoy on failure of characters of, 64–66

DATE DUE

GAYLORD   PRINTED IN U.S.A.